How best to use this blog

This is not an ordinary book. When you start reading it you will realise that it's in the form of a web log, albeit in book form. The reason it's not being distributed principally on a website is because I wanted to ensure anyone anywhere in any place or location can easily access it.

Here's why it's no ordinary 'how-to' book...

1. Written in plain simple conversational language
2. It's designed to be used on a DAILY basis over two months so you can build your success chunk by chunk
3. I repeat key concepts over the sixty days because I am coaching you rather than presenting information
4. It's based on taking some very simple actions. This alone will ensure successful outcomes

5. I have ensured there are a handful of fundamental principles here repeated in different forms, so following the daily approach really does work

6. Those people who have already tried this bit-by-bit approach *have reported amazing results...*

7. It's an easy read so that the emphasis is on getting on with your goals rather than getting stuck in deep and meaningful theory

Whether you have some great goals for the next sixty days or not, I dare you to start reading THE SIXTY DAY SUCCESS BLOG and carry out the very straightforward actions each and every day for the next two months. Then e-mail me your results at results@deanthorpe.com.

I intend to publish some of the best results stories in *The Sixty Day Success Blog – Revisited*

Foreword

For those of you who know anything about me, you will know that snooker is my life. From a child, I've always been passionate about the game and when I won the World Snooker Championship in 2005 it was the end point of a journey I started at the age of twelve.

Of course I was delighted to win and yet at the same time it was no real surprise. When you want something badly enough, and you're serious about achieving it everything else that comes after this tends to be the easy part.

For me it's snooker, for Dean it's been about creating a success model that's worked for him and will work for anyone who's also serious about achieving greatness in as little as 60 days.

I've enjoyed my association with Dean to date. We share much in the way we think and what we believe in. It's been a breath of fresh air to be a guest in front of some of Dean's audiences where I've had the pleasure of meeting individuals hungry for success in their own chosen fields.

I know this blog will change people's lives. It's packed with sixty instalments of daily goodies that anyone can follow and use. I for one have already started the sixty-day blog for the new goals I wish to achieve immediately and in the near future.

I would recommend the experience of high achievement to everyone and I'm delighted to endorse this marvellous success tool that you've invested in. Now invest in yourself, make today Day 1 and get going!

I know if you're serious, not only is this the doorway to creating positive change in your life, but also the start of a really enjoyable journey of discovery.

Shaun Murphy

World Snooker Champion 2005

Introduction

One of the most annoying things about being successful is when someone comes up to you and says, "Dean, you're so lucky!"

When I see what I've managed to achieve in my relatively short life to date, luck of course had nothing to do with it. I've always believed that luck is an excuse invented by losers. The day you ditch your four-leaf clover and don a driven attitude, an unquenchable thirst to materialise *exactly what you want*, is the day that your luck will change for the better and dare I say you become extremely lucky in just about every aspect of your life.

I've always maintained that success means different things to different people. What I may perceive to be successful you may disagree with and it's curious isn't it how you meet people with vast sums of money at their disposal who are completely miserable.

In my case, I have my own family business, own a home with all the trappings to make my immediate family comfortable, enjoy an extremely healthy income yet have the freedom to make money work for me not the other way around.

I also have the most wonderful family, a wife who I adore and children to die for. Yet with all this magic in place, I continue to have a healthy regard for the future and a desire to continue my success journey to even more wondrous places.

Over the years I've been inspired by books, events and people. They've all contributed to giving me what I needed to reach the point on the success ladder where I'm positioned today.

I'm also mindful of the old adage: "Those who can, do – and those who can't, teach or talk about it". I'd like to point out from the very beginning of this journey that I hope you're going to take with me, one of my dearest goals I've had inside me for many years is the conviction to help and support other people who would like to make more of their lives; yet for one reason or another have failed in their quest.

This is not me being egotistical or altruistic because it's the thing to do. It's a genuine gut-felt passion I have that truly does burn inside me. Hearing from people who complete this 60-day journey to greater achievement and win as a result, will automatically lift me to even higher levels of attainment and personal satisfaction on my own personal ongoing expedition.

If you thumb through my blog before buying it you will hopefully have noticed it's very practical. This is because any journey to success is three-dimensional. *It's about seeing, hearing, thinking and most of all <u>doing</u>.*

My blog will become the foundation for a blog of your own. Your 60-day set of success steps that culminate in the achievement you've yet to experience in your life. So when you make decisions about why, what, how, where and when – push the boat out. I dare you.

I've always considered that most humans fit in one of two categories: they are either intenders or non-intenders. If you purchase this book I am making the assumption that you are definitely an intender, someone who desperately wishes to achieve their wildest dreams in the smallest timeframe possible. I'm also hoping that you will settle for it in just 60 days...

Now you may be thinking, how can I achieve all my dreams in a mere 60 days? And that's a really good question.

For me a dream realised is a door in my mind opening on the aim or objective, as well as a clear set of 'can-do' steps that I am one hundred percent confident that I can follow to the full attainment of the goal. Many call this a breakthrough. I would call it your **dream breakthrough.** Imagine over the next 60 days achieving dream breakthroughs in everything you want. Would you not then feel successful? Creators of major businesses over the years have realised their ultimate objectives through **dream breakthroughs.** Companies like IBM and McDonald's started to make millions once the individual on that journey suddenly saw the future with absolute clarity. From that point onwards, the uphill challenge or even struggle became a downhill feet-in-the-air bicycle ride to where they wanted to go.

Whatever your hill or mountain is, I am inviting you to read my blog on a day-by-day basis. If you decide to read the entire book in one go, I cannot guarantee success. If you read it in daily instalments, (the way blogs work), and *take action* each day based on what've you've read before reading the next instalment, 60 days from now you're going to be in an amazing place.

Of course the other thought is – surely a blog or *web log* is online, not in a book. Aren't we going backwards here? Or is this a solution for the none too technical?

Neither.

What you're reading started out as my very own web log challenging myself to create a process for others to use. Within days of starting it, I realised that my number one goal was *to help others* and there I was using it principally for myself with the odd reference to readers. On day 4 I made a decision to write it purely for the benefit of others given I had already used the tools and techniques to great effect in my own business and life.

So each blog entry is one of 60 steps that I feel will create that cumulative effect where a step represents a day. And yes we're talking about the weekends as well!

I'm always amused when people say, "Do I have to work on my success over the weekends or can I have the time off?" That's a bit like being on a diet and always taking the weekends off where you binge and binge. That would be rather like being on a never-ending cycle of feast and famine. This 60-day experience is about feast, more feast and your ultimate feast. There will be challenges along the way, and my commitment is to ensure you never lose your way and always have a tool or two up your sleeve that will get you out of trouble should such an event occur. And being focused on what you want to achieve each day doesn't mean not taking time out. It's always good to have time to rest and replenish everything – physical and mental.

So here's the proposition:

You copy what I did for sixty days and go **from** 1 **to** 60, **from** deciding what **you want to achieve** *using the same process* – I imagine, substantial results in sixty days.

THE SIXTY DAY SUCCESS BLOG

You take some action every single day.

How much time you spend each day will be up to you though the minimum required will be ten minutes.

Yes, you can repeat a day if need be, yet I'm confident that you could still achieve greatness spending a mere 10-20 minutes each and every day for the full period.

If you miss a day, or worse still miss several days, you will still be required to pick things up from where you left off. Personally I think it will be a great shame if you ended up doing your sixty days over a period of several years. I'm sure you would agree that the effect and result is unlikely to be as exciting or indeed the same. There's a momentum that builds by doing a little often. It's a bit like exercise or dieting – a little done often goes an extremely long way.

Before heading for my first day's blog entry, be absolutely sure you are up for this. And even if you have doubts, the first few days are designed to put your mind in the right place.

Finally, before we begin, you may be wondering where all the content of this has come from. I really wish I could say it's all straight out of my head.

The reality is that I've gleaned a great deal from listening, studying, researching and asking other people. Some of these individuals I have met personally; others I have never met before but would like to and there are of course yet other individuals who are no longer with us who I've studied over the years. Sprinkled within this rich tapestry of information, I have been able to share some of my own thinking and experience. The combination of all of these things and people is what you are currently holding in your hands.

I wish you well on this journey and I promise to guide you to the best of my ability every step of the way over the next sixty days.

Here then is my Success Blog, dedicated to your desired achievements.

Dean Thorpe 2009

The 60-Day Success Blog

Day 1

"The more I learn, the more I realise how little I know... The more I want to know, the more I learn." (Albert Einstein).

The Journey begins...

Beginning...

Today's an exciting day.

This is the first day of the rest of our 60-day journey. Whatever we do today will to a large extent shape the final outcome so from my side I want to make sure I make a robust start to the way forward. A real opportunity to *really make dreams and desired goals a reality.*

For years I used to make plans around January for the new year ahead. Year after year I'd get disappointed. This often happened at the end of January.

I challenge you to work with me. And although strictly speaking a web log's online, think not of the medium we're using, but consider sixty bite-size chunks of inspiration to get you those goals that have been hanging around for far too long.

Your part in this, is to read one chunk a day and action my suggestions to the best of your ability. That's it. I promise to ensure each chunk is highly achievable.

Let's begin.

I'm imagining it's winter. I'm standing looking at an outdoor swimming pool that's not heated. I kneel at the side of it and put my hand into the water. It's freezing. Yet, as a swimmer I know that once I take the plunge and start swimming it will soon feel like heated water and I'll be enjoying the experience.

I'm assuming that you, the reader of my blog will know what you want to achieve in the next sixty days.

Having said that there will be some who are completely unsure of what it is they should be aiming for. If you're in this latter category I recommend you start by making a list, like a shopping list, and write down absolutely everything you want from the rest of your life.

Having done this, it would be an idea to select from the list the item or items that would make **dream breakthroughs** over the next sixty days.

I recommended some additional reading at the end of today's first blog entry too which may be of help.

When you know what you want

Now I'm going to use some of the work of Bernice McCarthy. This lady got to grips with the power of questions. And there's actually a questioning sequence that when used as a process around anything creates clarity of thought and impetus towards your journey. I've slightly extended the process here:

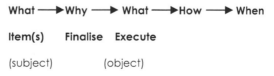

What ⟶ Why ⟶ What ⟶ How ⟶ When

Item(s)   Finalise   Execute

(subject)   (object)

Today I'm simply going to do the first part – namely the Why?

I want to apply the question 'why' to your goals for the next sixty days. Initially this might sound a little counterproductive. Surely if you do know what you want why would we need to question it?

That's because playing devil's advocate will help firm up your desire and the momentum the desire brings to enable you to go the full distance. So all I will ask you to do next is to write down fast and furiously as many reasons as possible as to why you want to do all that you're about to embark on.

By the way, if all you write is something on the lines of "I want to be successful" or "I want to make some money out of an idea" then I must strongly suggest you need to ask yourself some more 'why'.

In order to help you, here are some possible 'why' questions for you:

- Why are these goals particularly important to me over the next sixty days?
- Why have I chosen these ones specifically over other possible goals in my life?

- Why is achieving these goals first going to be most satisfying?
- Why do I want these things to happen soon?
- Why is achieving these goals going to make a big difference to me?
- Why does this give me a buzz? (If there's no buzz, again why am I doing it?)

I encourage you to put your deliberations into a specific file or notebook set aside for this project. When you're done on the above, you may pat yourself on the back for having achieved Day 1's blog suggestion from me.

That's it for day one. By the way, if you carry on in this fashion by simply following what I suggest you will suddenly find yourself at Day 60 joining me with a chilled glass of champagne and toasting that sweet smell of success.

Further recommended reading through the sixty days...

Being Happy! A Handbook to Greater Confidence and Security.

Day 2

"Learn it, love it, do it." (Tom Devine)

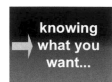

Sanity Check

Before we continue let's be very clear what's achievable in sixty days.

Naturally, it's not for me to outline what's possible and not so likely for you – you're the only one who can make this judgement.

For example, if you wanted to complete a university degree from start to finish in two months, then it's rather unlikely that this will happen. Equally if you wanted to set up your own business from scratch and already have a deposit in place, then although you may have never done it before you'll be staggered what's achievable in such a short time frame.

So along with all your 'why' questions, ensure you are applying these questions to a worthy goal or goals.

Part of the psychology of this process is for you to make some real headway fast, perhaps for the first

time in your life. Therefore this push forward might be part of a really large goal or goals. So let's imagine that your big goal is building your own house, these next two months might be about the success in scoping the project, raising the capital, finding the right architect who comes up with the goods, locating the right piece of land, negotiating and striking a bargain with your purchase so that you end up ready to lay the first brick.

For most of us, we live our lives and we end up with elements of regret. Regret invariably originates from our early beliefs in what we can and can't do. These are indeed no more than beliefs and with every belief there is an underlying possibility for a lie to be contained within. Indeed if you look at the word

'belief' you will see the three letters that create this word staring back at you.

Yesterday we started to identify goals and ask why questions, Here's another why question:

Why don't you make this 60-day trip your most successful attempt ever in getting ahead and staying there?

Your task today is to write up your final goals list in index cards. Bear in mind that each one you write must be achieved, so only write what you want to complete on. For big audacious goals, you may want to write down what would create a **dream breakthrough.**

Day 3

"Brains like hearts go where they are appreciated."
(Robert S. McNamara)

The Monitoring System

So today's about setting up a monitoring system that you'll be using from tomorrow onwards. Before I go into this I'd also like to confirm that we've now got one or more index cards with goals to achieve on them. Having dealt with the 'why' we soon need to explore the 'what' in more depth.

Putting together a Monitoring System

By monitoring system I'm referring to a diary but not any old diary. Yes, you could simply have a book and make notes every day or you could be a little bit more creative.

How about having a recording device such as a dictaphone and downloading your thoughts verbally each and every day? You could choose a software option like Quicktime and do this as an audio or video. You could even use a mobile phone and Bluetooth daily blogs to a PC or laptop.

Another option is a video camera on a tripod and every day, using a remote, recording yourself for a minute or two.

I would encourage you to use some sort of easy-to-film title so that, who knows, one day you may wish to replay all sixty entries over a few hours and relive your success story. If you go the video route, then in a way you're also making a documentary and you will need to record the good the bad and the ugly regardless.

Recording your journey using technology suddenly makes this a serious enterprise, which is exactly where your mind needs to be. You must decide what's right for you.

So go arrange your monitoring system after reading through your goals on index cards one more time.

What is vitally important is to keep a day-to-day record. Today is about sorting this out.

Day 4

"Catch them doing it approximately right." (Ken Blanchard)

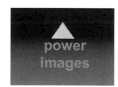

Power Images

Let's start today by confirming the great potential in creating... ***Dream Breakthroughs.***

Today I want you to get onto the Internet and Google. Once there I want you to find images that relate to your goals, and save them. As many as you can find, though only spend up to fifty minutes, no more.

What about the "What?"

Okay, so it's time for some 'what' questions.

You may be thinking, "but I know what I want now". Great, today's making sure you've made the right choices.

Here are some possible questions:

- What **exactly** do I want to achieve from your listed goals. What **detail** have you thought through?
- What will the outcome of achieving these things lead to **after** day 60?
- What have I failed to achieve on these lines before that I should **avoid** this time?
- What **prerequisites** do I need in place right now before going any further?
- What will change in my life when I've achieved my dream breakthroughs?

- And most important. **What goal or part of a goal should I ignore because I don't really want that? (I just think I do).**

<u>Summary for today</u>

Get onto the Internet and Google

De-clutter your list. Remove anything you're not truly passionate about achieving.

Quick what test: Does the item make you *excited*? If not, remove it from the list.

Your diary entry today should convince you and anyone else watching/reading/listening to it that you're really on the right trail and know **what you want.**

Catch you tomorrow.

Day 5

"Reflect back (to your team) the best they can be... give them a reputation to live up to." (Simon Twigger – Sainsburys)

Today? It's about the How.

• **HOW?**

We're getting down to the nitty-gritty.

I'd like you to explore **how** you intend to achieve your goal(s) which are 55 days away now.

So let's check out the 'how':

• How are you going to go about moving forward from this moment on? (The next steps for each goal?)
• How are you feeling about them right now?
• How can you make the rest of the journey **easier?**
• How will you deal with any challenges along the way? (How's your mindset?)

In order to help with the how, I suggest you get a sheet of paper and make three columns. Firstly *what I can absolutely do*, secondly *what I can do with help* and finally *what I can do by taking a risk.*

Let's look at these three things.

The first column is very straightforward. There should be nothing stopping you taking these actions which I fully expect you to do. The second column simply needs a bit of thought, a few calls and some alignment with others. Finally it's the final column that will make the biggest difference. There's an old Red Indian proverb.

'Man who fish in rapids gets more fish than man who fishes in shallows where most other men fish...'

I am going to suggest that what you do from your choices in column three will make the **biggest difference** in helping you achieve your desired outcomes.

Today you must make your decision on what you will do in terms of *how you do it.*

Make your choice, and create your ongoing strategy. Diarise actions if need be, then make your daily blog entry. If you don't know the how, keep going. There are lots more tools coming up.

Day 6

"Change is rarely a matter of ability, it's almost always a matter of motivation." (Sir John Harvey Jones)

Milestones

Today, having answered your 'hows' now go on to ask yourself where and when?

'Where' is only appropriate around location questions and once you've answered the first 'where' question, you may wish to come in with 'why' questions and 'how' questions around your answer.

Since you've had three days of asking questions you should be a bit of a dab hand now at seeing the power of good questions from different perspectives and angles.

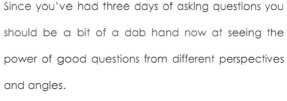

Finally go on to 'when' which is about time and deadlines.

We already know there is a sixty-day structure to this project and you are now on Day 6. Given this, you may wish to create mini-milestones along the way as measures for success.

THE SIXTY DAY SUCCESS BLOG

Day 7

Everyone thinks of changing the world, but no one thinks of changing himself." (Leo Tolstoy)

I'm fully aware over the last few days that some of the questions you might have found hard to answer or indeed maybe you've not been able to answer at all.

At this point I'd like to draw your attention to the resource mind maps at the end of the book. Whenever you come to a point at which you feel you are in a 'cul-de-sac', then look at the resource page on Solution-Finding as I'm confident there will always be something there to get you back on the road again.

Please download your thoughts for today using your monitoring system as usual. From now on I will assume you automatically do this every day.

If you're struggling with your daily blog it means one of two things:

1. You're not taking enough action
2. You've not chosen the right goals which get you excited enough.

If you need to, you have to address these two things before tomorrow. And, congratulations you've completed your first week and we're still moving forward.

The task for today is writing a paragraph about how you succeeded. Imagine it's Day 60 and you achieved all of it. Whatever you'd record on that day, record that now.

Day 8

"If you always do what you've always done, you'll always get what you've always got." (Albert Einstein)

Phone a Friend

Having answered all the relevant questions, it's time to put some meat on the bone. All I want you to do today is to telephone a close friend and share what you're doing with them.

However, please choose this person well. Choosing the wrong person might mean your time invested so far could be torn apart by someone who can only see what's wrong with what you're doing rather than what's right with it. If you're having difficulty thinking of someone suitable then confine your thoughts purely to your monitoring system.

Though we've spent seven days on creating the direction, I hope you will agree that it's been important to chunk it out so that we've given your subconscious an opportunity to do some evaluation work devoid of any pressure.

When you make this call to a friend today or extended blog entry, use the short sentences and/or key words to express what's going on for you. Be positive, optimistic and talk about the outcome as if there's no chance you'll fail. Though you appear to be chatting to a friend, you'll also be talking to someone else. Your subconscious mind. In fact you're affirming your journey now. Miss out today's requirement and you'll do just that... miss out.

Above all, have fun doing it!

Day 9

"The very essence of Leadership is that you have to have a vision... You cannot blow an uncertain trumpet." (Jack Welch)

Finding the Best of the best

We have already looked at some detail. Let's finalise on this today.

Option 1 – Putting together some finer details

If a detailed plan is essential complete with financials (if it's about a business), then we need to get this in place next.

Of course this might be something that will take several days and you will need to squeeze it in doing a little at a time until it's complete. Equally you might want to delegate this task to someone like an accountant who could be working alongside you at the same time.

If you feel you need more information – take some action today to make this happen.

Option 2-Detailed plan not essential

If no detailed plan is required then what you'll have so far is a good idea of how it's going to pan out over the next few months and possibly some milestones in place.

How I will continue to help you

How we move this forward is that every day I will continue to give you tips, tools and techniques to advance the achievement of your ideal outcomes. Of course what you might glean on Day 11 you may not need until Day 46. Equally something you are missing during Days 27 to 29 could pop up on Day 35. In other words my job is to ensure that ultimately you have everything you need. Should you ever find yourself in a corner with no escape route then you may wish to play your ace card. I refer to my e-mail address.

If you're desperate e-mail me via www.deanthorpe.com and I will do my best to offer some personal helpful advice.

Today I want you to identify people who have succeeded in the goal or goals you wish to achieve, and then contact them for help and advice.

Let's imagine you want to become a volleyball champ. Who are the leading players in your part of the country? How can you contact them? If not the top players, who else could you contact – who could help you equally or get you in touch with the best of the best?

Day 10

"The best leaders should be judged on the results they have achieved and the number of leaders they have helped develop." (Anthony Robbins)

---

shifting into a higher gear

Preparing to Shift into a Higher Gear

Time flies.

I remember receiving an e-mail from someone who'd started the 60 days and around now had still not fully articulated what she wanted.

She contacted me to ask whether she could put everything on hold and continue Day 9 after she'd spent a few months thinking through her desired objectives.

I'm sure you can guess what my answer was!

If we revert to the swimmer analogy, what's happened is that she's jumped into the cold pool, is feeling uncomfortable and wants to get out, dry herself and think about whether she really wants to continue her swim.

The more appropriate and successful approach should be that now you're in the pool keep kicking the water behind you and soon you'll find a rhythm and motivation that will take you all the way.

Having said this, to test whether you have enough to really continue the journey I'd like you to create the following:

- A movie title
- A lift statement
- A tag line

about your most **important goal.**

1. The Movie Title

If you were going to call your journey or overall goal the name of a movie, either well-known or completely new out of your head, what would the movie be called?

If you're not a particularly visual person you might like to do this assuming it's the title of a book. This may appear an unusual thing to do and I can guarantee it really clarifies your thinking. Have a go and see what you come up with.

2. The Lift Statement

Having a 'lift statement' is about having a sentence by which you can apply the essence of where you're headed. You may have done this already when constructing your detailed plan and either this is repetition of the same or you may wish to revise or renew it completely.

So, if you were in the lift with somebody and they turned and said to you, "So what are you currently aiming for in your life? What would your reply be?

3. Tag Line

If your journey or overall goal was a tag line, a bit like having a few words under your product that's off to market what would the tag line be?

I always remember one client who was desperate to set up his own business as a fashion photographer. In going through this process he quickly came up with the following two tag lines for his business:

- Photographing the bold and the beautiful
- I love to capture inspirational facial landscapes

When I got these by e-mail I could instantly see what he was after and where he was going as these elements created strong vivid pictures in my mind. As you know from the classic quotation, a single picture is worth a thousand words.

Question Summary

Lots of questions have been asked since we began, and I think it an idea to have a summing up – a making sure you can answer everything you need to. So here we go:

- What do you want?
- Why do you want it?
- How will you know when you've got it?
- Where, when and with whom do you want it?
- What would the result do for you?
- Is there anything you may lose as a result of attaining what you want?
- How will attainment affect your lifestyle?
- Would the new situation be an improvement?
- What are you prepared to do about it?
- What would happen if you never pursued what you now want to achieve?
- What's stopped you in the past?
- Why won't this be a barrier any more?
- What's important to you in your goal(s) achievement?

- Are you willing to go to any length to achieve what you most desire?

- Are you expecting problems along the way?

- Are you prepared to confront and deal with any problems?

Day 11

"Creating an environment in which your people can and want to flourish." CEO of Pharmacia

---

Starting a 1-2-3

From today you'll be starting a daily 1-2-3.

These are three actions I want you to aim to achieve each and every single day.

Your 1-2-3 consists of three types of daily action. Let's look at the first two.

Bold actions

Quite simply these are things that you know you need to achieve to get you nearer your goals.

Resistant actions

These are things which you are probably going to struggle to complete because there's a strong possibility you dislike these things.

They appear boring to do or you would just rather someone else did them!

Of course in this category the chances are you're very clear that all of these items need to be done by you yourself. (I think it's important to note here that delegation is always a good thing and if you can delegate small tasks, then of course by all means do so.)

Today, decide on your daily BOLD and RESISTANT goals, then achieve them.

Day 12

"Leaders are made, they are not born. They are made by hard effort." (Vince Lombardi)

Breakthrough time

How did you get on with your two goals from yesterday?

Now let's set up the third part of your daily 1-2-3.

Breakthrough Actions

These are things which, if you achieve them, you'll be over the moon, often achieving a significant breakthrough.

So the way 1-2-3 works is you pick one item from each list and ensure they are carried out to the letter each and every day right up to Day 60.

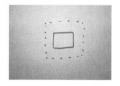

Whether or not I make mention of your 1-2-3, I am assuming that you are starting this process in earnest TODAY and consistently thereafter.

Day 13

Logic will get you from A to B, imagination will get you everywhere else." (Albert Einstein)

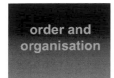

Order and Organisation

All top achievers are more likely to have order and organisation in their mind and/or in their life compared with those non-achievers who seem to favour chaos and confusion.

It's fascinating visiting people's offices for example. I'll go into someone's office that's neat and tidy, where everything has its place and I guarantee you that this person is moving forward.

Equally, I often get told all sorts of stories about an individual's success and yet what they're saying absolutely doesn't match the state of their office, which is sadly a reflection of their disordered mind and thinking.

You can of course do this the other way around.

By forcing yourself to have order and organisation in everything you do the chances are it's going to affect the clarity of your thinking which in turn will modify and change the nature and quality of the success you're yearning for.

So here are some suggestions:

- Do a massive DE-CLUTTER as soon as possible. Throw out every clothing item you've not worn for six months. (Naturally this won't apply to things like dinner jackets and evening wear.)

- De-clutter both your office and home or just the latter if you don't have an office. It's highly unlikely that you'll be able to do this all today, so plan how you can get this done. My suggestion is that you allocate certain dates/times in your diary today, then stick to the agreed slots. The sooner you de-clutter the better. In order to make this really successful, you must be absolutely ruthless. I often get great surprises from people who undertake this process with real energy and conviction. A de-cluttered existence creates a clear, sharp and focused mind which is critical for any would-be achiever. Personally, when I first heard this as an idea I was sceptical, yet I have been amazed just how much it has helped me.

Minimalism and Clarity

So how tidy are you? Some would say that creative people are quite untidy and that the untidiness helps them to come up with ideas. If this works for you then fine, however if at the moment you would like to be more creative and feel less stressed in your life you might want to go minimal or at least have a massive clear-out. Clean lines in your home and in your office, wherever that might be, with as little paper as possible and as few things surrounding you as possible undoubtedly removes stress. Stress after all is highly psychological and can attack you consciously or subconsciously. One of the subconscious factors of stress is disorder, untidiness and quite simply clutter.

Since you started the journey in this book, what have you done to create better order and organisation in your life? Today I would like to invite you to create even more order and organisation in your life by spending a little time throwing away as many things as possible that you no longer need (you may wish to put them on eBay!). You will find that the greater the space that surrounds you and the less clutter, the less stressed and more motivated you're likely to feel. One way of experimenting with this idea is to take this approach in one room. By all means have plenty of clutter everywhere else in the house, yet when entering this one room what you will see is order, organisation and a sense of minimalism. My strong recommendation is that after doing this in one room and seeing the instant benefit every time you walk in, you do the same with the rest of your home. This should also be extended to your car and any other places that are linked to you.

Day 14

"As long as you are going to be thinking, think BIG."
(Donald Trump)

Emerging Mindset

The next three days is about mindset.

Much has been written about the subject, particularly over the last fifty years in the vast and ever-growing personal development marketplace.

Since the late 70s there has been a huge amount of both audio and visual material concerning personal transformation. Many individuals and organisations have made big contributions to this vast arena and dare I say here I am offering my very own contribution in this blog.

My only concern is that many people often read across the page rather than down the page. Let me explain. I have a friend who prides himself on being really up-to-date with all the personal development books and he often boasts about the number of personal transformation seminars he's attended over the years.

Yet when I look at his life he's singularly unsuccessful. He resides in a house that needs desperate redecoration, he's always short of money to make his life more exciting, and he's ever complaining about how things are not working out for him and how it's never his fault – always someone else's.

When I've tried to help him, it has included offering assistance in certain DVDs and books that have inspired me to bigger and better things. Invariably he takes these materials, reads them and then rings me up to tell me that he's heard much of this already.

This guy's reading *across the pages*. What I really want him to do is to read down the page, in other words with depth of understanding.

It's one thing understanding a concept superficially, as in reading across the page; it's quite something else putting the understanding into practical action as near to immediately as possible.

It's this second thing that he's simply not doing and sadly has never done seriously in his life. I've even tried to explain the difference between reading across the page and down the page to him and it's like water off a duck's back.

Today I want you to watch, buy (to watch), borrow (to watch) or stream a copy (to watch) of THE SECRET. The website is thesecret.tv. Not the book. The DVD version. If you've seen it before, watch it again.

Day 15

How was THE SECRET? No big secret – the Law of Attraction, though it's true many people have not known about it before. The missing part is the plan after watching it. The action part. And that's what I'm providing. More about the Law of Attraction further into the book.

So we're discussing mindset and its importance. Each one of us has a mind shielded by three major types of filter. These filters are:

- Deletion
- Generalisation
- Distortion

Whenever information hits our brain we invariably use these filters to ensure that what we're hearing and seeing which equates to thinking, matches our beliefs. If it fails to match our belief we will change the information so it does match. The sum total of this experience I refer to as our personal set of beliefs.

Each of us has a mindset slightly different in nature. Like a fingerprint it is very much something we've moulded as our own over time. The majority of humans have a predilection for a more negative way of thinking and a minority of humans much prefer an optimistic outlook attached to just about everything they think about.

You won't be surprised to know that unless you can ensure your thinking is positive and optimistic you are unlikely to achieve the success over the forty-five days that remain from tomorrow.

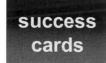

Success cards

Today, alongside your daily 1-2-3 today I'd like you to write out sixteen success cards.

You already have index cards with your desired goals. This is taking this to the next stage.

On each card is a goal that you want to achieve by the end of the sixty-day period and it's written as a sentence or a couple of sentences on a new index card. You should have up to 16.

Ideally write the goal in the past or present tense but never in the future tense. For example, if your goal is to set up a computer system for your new business idea you might write down:

Isn't it great having a computer system which makes my business much more effective and profitable?

Or

The computer system we used in the business that we sold for over a million pounds was the bedrock of our success.

Can you see how this works?

Once you've got your sixteen cards I want you to read them every day. Over time you can add cards so you ultimately have at least thirty. Then simply continue to read them every day. When a card happens, collect it and add a new card with a new goal. This is a very simple idea and highly effective which over the years has been used by some of the most successful people.

If you want to really make this idea zing, use a PowerPoint Presentation or Keynote Speaker if you're on Apple. Add some pictures and music, then press play once a day. Now that's what today is about. Setting up a visual mindset that ideally you can **play once a day.**

Day 16   *"The beginnings of all things are small." (Cicero)*

---

check the roadmap

Checking the Roadmap so far...

Let's clarify where we are.

- You've embarked on a journey with me and have spent several days creating clarity on why, what, how, when and where. Each day you're undertaking three goals – your 1-2-3.
- You have sixteen goal cards which you're reading every day confirming what's important to you.
- You're working from a plan or detailed notes.

- You've shared your dreams and ambitions with a friend and will continue to do so on and off in the future until you get to your final destination.
- You're aware of resource mind maps at the end of this book if you get stuck.
- You've read 'Being Happy!' and seen The Secret.
- You're still excited and raring to go for the rest of the journey.

You're already using the Success Cards System and have sixteen written out. I would like you now to increase this to twenty-two. It's important that some of these cards are definitely personal goals rather than simply related to career/business or work. In fact it's good to have a balance between project goals and goals of a more general and personal nature. Once again, the total number of cards need to be read once every day.

Day 17

"Minds are like parachutes, they only function when open." (Thomas Dewar)

Seeing More Results Now

Eyes closed visuals

Find a comfortable chair in a quiet place, sit and relax completely then shut your eyes. From now on every day I'd like you to do this for up to three minutes. With your eyes shut imagine, with as many senses as possible, how things will be with your ultimate goal achieved. See what you see, hear what you hear, and feel what you feel. If you can imagine the sense of smell or taste where appropriate add that into the recipe too. Always see it as having been achieved so it comes across as real rather than something you desire and therefore simply wished for.

Eyes open visuals

For at least a couple of minutes every day I'd also like you to do the same thing with your eyes wide open. Many people find that the eyes open version is often stronger than doing this with your eyes shut – hence

slightly less time required. This is very akin to daydreaming. Though we're often told to wake up and stop dreaming, it's probably more appropriate for it to be the other way around, namely wake up and start dreaming. Though I've already explained that we're not making pictures of something wished for, it's quite acceptable to see your dream in its completed achieved state while you focus at a point around you.

Also choose a symbol you can have stuck around your home, office, car and so on. For example, a gold star. This symbolises success at school so would be a good choice. You can buy a set of sticky gold stars from a stationers. Don't go mad, but do stick the odd star where you will catch sight of it. You may also carry a star in your purse or wallet. Now look into the star you carry at least once a day. Visualise with clarity what you want to create. Whenever you also catch sight of the other stars, even though momentarily, you can help be reminded of your goal – on a regular basis throughout the day. A very simple idea, that works.

THE SIXTY DAY SUCCESS BLOG

A client I coached used blue dots. He purchased a page of adhesive blue spots from a stationers and then placed them around his home, car and office. He would also carry a blue spot on a piece of card in his wallet. Once a day he would take out the card, look at the blue spot and do this technique with his eyes wide open. As he looked into the miniature blue TV screen as it were, he saw his objectives as well-formed outcomes. It's extraordinary how we have the ability to programme our minds to hunt and retrieve precisely what we desire in our lives. It's just that we fail to use some very simple processes to help us get there, given that when we were born we never got the instruction manual that goes with our mind!

Day 18

"Curiosity is one of the most permanent and certain characters of a vigorous intellect." (Samuel Johnson)

Today's concept is called six of the best. I'd like you to look at your future plan and skim through your diary entries to date and identify the six critical areas you need to achieve to enjoy the success you're looking for by the end of the sixty days.

For example, if your ultimate goal is to create the most amazing website, your six of the best might be:

1.   Complete specification for designer
2.   More research for the site
3.   Marketing plan to launch site
4.   Content is king – ensure content is extraordinary
5.   Credit card and payment systems in place for the launch
6.   Legals and regulations around the new business

Even if your project isn't a website, it's likely you'll still have a different set of six things that you want to focus on. Let's now take this opportunity of you thinking of what these six things are for your project. Please note that if you can't think of six things that's fine and it shouldn't exceed six things. If you have too long a list of topics then very often your subconscious tends to switch off. So today's key task is to come up with your six of the best.

You may also like to think about your six of the best for life as a whole. What are the six key most important areas of your life? For many people it would be things like finances, health, career, friends, family, goals, wish list and so on. If you don't have such a list anywhere you might consider creating it today alongside your six of the best for your project.

The Lack of Goals in the World

Though people talk about goals incessantly in their lives, few people actually set them and even fewer set and get them. I'd like you to think about this for a moment. First of all, how many goals have you ever set in your life? Are you somebody who believes that a goal has to be big, broad and incredibly worthy? Or are you someone who sees goals more like a shopping list of mini items that are 'nice to haves'. I'm going to suggest to you that the word itself will remind you of what an ideal goal should be.

Gratifying

Outrageous

Action-orientated

Leads you forward

Though it sounds rather obvious, a goal should be gratifying otherwise why would you want to have it? It should also be specifically gratifying so there's absolutely no doubt what you're aiming for. I'm amazed when people tell me that their goal is, for example, to *lose some weight*. Months later they say to me that they are no further forward in their quest. Now had they declared that their goal was:

to lose ten pounds by August 3rd in order to look toned and healthy for my beach holiday...

this would then present us with a completely different ball game altogether.

Think of your subconscious as a little child, a child that will absorb 100% of what you tell them then act upon it. Of course you have to be wary that this child will indeed replicate your message, whether it be positive or negative. Like all children, they get excited by positive and inspirational images. They're more likely to do their utmost for you if your message is upbeat, ambitious and creates instant appeal.

Having outrageous goals is also important. Sometimes the more outrageous the goal, the greater the impetus and inner drive there is. In the Sixties, Americans were in awe when John F Kennedy announced that America was planning to launch a spacecraft and land on the moon for the first time. Many people today affirm that it was his announcement and the way he delivered the message that inspired NASA and other groups to go all out on their outrageous mission. If you think about it, back in the early Sixties it was completely outrageous... At a time when computer science was in its infancy three humans were safely conveyed to the lunar surface and successfully returned back to Earth. Kennedy might have been forgiven for hedging his bets and simply announcing a series of moon shots without any hint of an actual moon landing being part of the agenda.

Have you never ever set out to do something outrageously successful? If you haven't, perhaps now's the time and if you have, particularly if you've achieved it, why haven't you made it something you do regularly?

The other essential ingredient in creating a great goal is that it's action-orientated. That's why simply *'lose some weight'* is fundamentally flawed. It's a wish rather than an action-orientated, gratifying and to some extent outrageous target to achieve.

The last part of the goal-setting formula is *leads you forward*. When you set a goal, is it in some way creating leverage and leading the way from one or more of the following perspectives:

- Leading your life in a new direction
- Leading the field against competition
- Leading you to new discoveries
- Leading others to a place that they thank you for
- Leading you to create something fresh and original

That's why it's quite ridiculous to set a goal for the day like *having lunch* or *buying yourself a treat* because these things are surely easy to achieve or are going to happen anyway. Any goal you set must lead the way and if it doesn't it's not a goal, simply a reminder or an action you're going to take regardless.

Day 19

"What helps luck is a habit of watching for opportunities, of having a patient, but restless mind, of sacrificing one's ease or vanity, and pressing through hard times bravely and cheerfully." (Victor Cherbuliez)

Location, location, location

Welcome to another instalment towards your sixty-day success opportunity to change your life. So how are you doing? Did you achieve your 1-2-3 yesterday? Did you do your mindset techniques? Are you completely up to date with your daily diary?

Today I want to talk about location and before I do let me also give you a final mindset idea, given that your attitude will continue to play a major part in your final drive to achieve 'nirvana'. Some of us prefer to be quite visual; others depend more on what they hear and a third category of human engages significantly on how they feel about things. Whichever your preference happens to be, all of us at some point will visualise things to a greater or lesser extent. My suggestion is that you start to cut out pictures from magazines, newspapers and from the Internet – visuals that inspire you towards your objective. Go to

any young budding football star's bedroom and I bet you anything you like the walls of the bedroom will be adorned with pictures of football, footballers and every type of football image. If your subconscious is subjected to living, eating and breathing images on a day-by-day basis it inevitably becomes that image in one way or another. Many might suppose that the images follow the success in that area, though if you think about it it's nearly always the other way around.

So I am suggesting you engage in this process by either getting a scrapbook or large sheet of paper upon which you can start collecting inspirational images that you'll see at least two or three times a week.

I always remember the story of one very visual man. Many years ago one of his goals was to own a Ferrari, so much so that he started to collect pictures of Ferraris and he even got his children involved, telling his son that he was going to be driving around in Dad's Ferrari very soon. He was doing this in order to get his subconscious onside so that he could acquire one. Things then started to spiral and one day he went to his son's school to be greeted by a teacher who congratulated him on his new Ferrari! This was slightly embarrassing as he had to explain that though he was hoping to have one soon he hadn't actually acquired one as yet. However curiously, not long after this somewhat embarrassing situation, seemingly completely out of the blue, a friend of a friend explained that he had a Ferrari for sale which he viewed and purchased. It's all about telling yourself what you want, and reminding yourself on a consistent regular basis until there's no choice but to deliver the goods in their entirety.

Now let's look at Location.

1. Location for your 'control centre'.

If you haven't already done so, I'd like you to select somewhere in your home or office where you keep your diary, and all matters relating to this journey we're on. It would also be prudent to have lots of images near and around your strategic place. If it's a desk then I would imagine you have a computer and/or paper-based system plus your monitoring device. Also at this location are all matters pertaining to your project neatly filed in a way you have instant access to whatever is required.

In my own control centre because its personal, I chose my home study rather than my business office. It's here I wrote my 60 days success blog. The location added to my successful outcome in the shape of this book. Interestingly my main period of inspiration came after I'd de-cluttered my study area (remember Day 14 Order & Organisation) and created a tidier working area which at the same time meant that I'd cleared my mind of clutter too.

2. A special location or retreat

This is a place that you go to get creative, motivated or inspired. For me, there's a particular golf course I like playing on and when I'm up against things and need some creative stimulation I take myself there for a round of golf or a coffee in the pavilion overlooking the first tee. It's an 'anchor' if you like... that anchors me to good positive thoughts, associations and vibes. Given that I've done a lot of my planning there as well as my strategies and my creative work on given projects which have turned out to be successful, it's the perfect place to go when something needs attention. So decide where your special place is and frequent it solely when you want that lift or burst, particularly when life throws a spanner in the works. Also remember that if there were no spanners thrown in your direction occasionally then your journey would be quite dull, boring and so very highly predictable.

3. Location for celebration

It's also a good idea to decide now where you're going to celebrate the success of your project of making some breakthroughs or turning your fortunes around. Whatever you are dedicating these 60 days towards in other words. If it's a restaurant who will you invite and might it be an idea to book a table immediately? Perhaps it's a weekend away and once more would you be prepared to be one hundred percent committed and book some flights or train tickets today?

It will also be very motivational knowing that you are going to be in a certain place on Day 60 and indeed to ensure that on this special day you at least have time available to rejoice in the success of your quest.

Finally, making arrangements to invite people along now is really sticking your neck out. Have you got the courage? Or are you simply toying with the potential of personal success.

I once had someone who did this in quite a big way. He told me that in order to celebrate the positive result of his sixty-day success plan he was going to fly to New York and have a haircut! Apparently, being a John Lennon fan, he was going to have a haircut at exactly the same place that John Lennon used to frequent in the late Seventies. It was indeed a great shame that halfway through his plan he failed to keep his promise to book the flight to New York, thinking that it was somewhat of an extravagance and it was no surprise thereafter that he never achieved his objective. I genuinely believe that when he cancelled the flight he cancelled the support of his subconscious, which as a child of his soul, was very much looking forward to the trip, and so withdrew.

Today – take the plunge. Make the booking. You know you need to. It will make the difference.

Day 20

"You have to expect things of yourself before you can do them." (Michael Jordan)

The Chicken List

Today I'd like you to take a long hard look at what you've achieved in the last nineteen days and ask yourself the question as to whether you are entirely happy with your results. Very often we are held back by doing the most obvious things because of an aversion or mental reason as to why we'd preferred not to take certain actions – hence the creation of a 'Chicken List' today.

This is a list of things that you absolutely know you have to achieve yet for one reason or another are not fully prepared to engage in. There are various ways of dealing with the list once it's been written. Three things to consider now:

- Use your 1-2-3 system, particularly daily goal 2 – your Resistant Goal to identify items for the list
- Also create mindset cards around some of your top chicken list goals to help make them happen

- Remind yourself of what you'd achieve by taking the plunge and just doing what you need to do, be it make a call, visit a place or person and so on.

Whenever we think of doing anything the pure thought is always balanced by the little voice in our head, often referred to as interference. This has been often noticed in the world of sports and you may like to read Timothy Gallwey's account of this in the *Inner Game of Tennis* written well over twenty years ago. He discovered that sports people are often put off their stroke by that little voice telling them something contrary to the desire or goal they wish to achieve. Imagine in a football match a striker who's about to go for a penalty kick. As he surges towards the ball seeing a picture of him striking the ball squarely, the little voice in his head might say to him, "Here we go again, you missed the last time!"

This is why players on many thousands of pounds per week still miss the entire goal area to the gasp of disbelief in the crowd and the inevitable endless self-deprecation for the player after the match.

So in every thought there is a potential element of interference producing a result which is determined by the winning agent in the mental formula. In other words if there is too much negative interference with the thought then the result is likely to be unsuccessful. Whereas, if the interference is tamed by the strength of a positive thought, then the result is equally positive. Some of the ways of dealing with interference is as simple as telling the voice to "be quiet!" This sounds a little ridiculous and yet can work quite effectively. Equally, interference can be subdued by regular mindset techniques that have already been outlined. Interference is purely a belief that fires off at the most inappropriate times. This also occurs when we are unaware of what's going on. Another word for an accepted belief creating interference is a 'paradigm'. The world is full of paradigms and you yourself are a collection of paradigms which make up your core beliefs and values. Paradigms can be good or bad and choosing the right ones will undoubtedly affect the end result in any situation.

Changing your Paradigms

Let's take an example of a paradigm that most humans have around the words 'bad news'. Imagine if you changed your paradigm to not accept that bad news existed. Let's suppose for a moment that you were to eliminate this phrase from your thinking and instead see all news as either good or neutral. I have done this from time to time and find the effect quite staggering. Someone rings me up and says to me, "Dean, I have some bad news". I don't know about you but that's not the most exciting thing to hear over the telephone from anyone. It triggers despondency and an expected 'low' in your mood. If you allow it to continue you are likely to believe that what you're hearing is bad news and react accordingly. You now have to go through the process of dealing with whatever it is and getting yourself out of the dip as soon as possible.

So why go through all of this? Now when someone in a day-to-day business context says to me I have some bad news, I correct them on the spot. I say to them, "Hang on. Let me be the judge of whether it's good or bad just say what it is". The reason why this approach works so well is that over the years people have delivered so-called bad news to me which actually turns out to be some of the best news that I've ever received.

Take for example a friend of mine who used to be a driving instructor and lost his licence. On the surface of this you may assume that this is catastrophic. The result of this so-called bad news was that the guy had to find an alternative career and ended up doing something that he'd always wanted. When pushed into the situation because of losing his licence he actually ended up better off both financially and mentally. In his new life in South Africa working with the local government in a project for disadvantaged children, he's never been more focused and fulfilled in all his life.

So the word 'bad' is purely subjective in any situation, is a judgement that you can choose to see an advantage in. The old adage *every cloud has a silver lining* is remarkably true. Eliminating using negative words and stopping people in their tracks using it in your direction is what I want you to give some thought to today and make it a new habit. There are some who use the word 'challenging' rather than bad or refer to a change of situation (a problem to many), as an 'opportunity'.

Continuing to move forward

I trust you will have an amazing day today and enjoy creating an outstanding diary entry. Here's continuing to wish you every success as we move towards Day 21.

Day 21

"A ship in the harbour is safe, but that's not what ships are for." (John Shed)

Windows of Opportunity

As you work through each day using your success tools to date I'd like to remind you that it's important to do everything you can to ensure your daily goals are dealt with in the following manner:

THE SIXTY DAY SUCCESS BLOG

- What you commit to you tackle to the best of your ability

- You never commit to things that you have little or no chance of ever achieving just because it sounds exciting

- Should you for any reason not achieve what you set out to do, you instantly arrange for it to be tacked on to another 1-2-3 set of goals as soon as possible.

- You ensure that you are stretching yourself with your goal setting and never making it so easy that it undermines your achievement.

Windows of Opportunity

Today's the day for a brainstorm session. I want you to open your address book and make a list of the most influential people you know. Then decide who you will call to ask for assistance to achieve your goals. These people may know others of course, and if you don't ask you don't get. The slight challenge with this, is that you may overlook those people you know who you think can't help you, so do really consider your choice with care and thought. It doesn't have to be telephone calls, you could equally e-mail people.

So if you want content for this new website business you're about to launch as an example, it's not going to come your way by chance. It does require some research and then making calls, writing letters and crafting e-mails to as many people as possible, often chasing your messages along the way to ensure they hit the mark. This also requires some good old-fashioned proactivity on your part where you take the bull by the horns and you create your future by solid and constructive actions. You can imagine how motivating it is to receive calls and messages from friends giving you good news in one form or another. It's the catalyst in the chemical reaction or the cream in the coffee. All it requires is some foresight, planning and physical movement on your part. Action is the key.

So your task today is to take some action. Even if it's one call to someone, I'd like you to identify this possibility and put the wheels into motion. Simple, straightforward and potentially hugely rewarding.

Day 22

"This is the true joy in life, the being used for a purpose recognized by yourself as a mighty one; the being thoroughly worn out before you are thrown on the scrap heap; the being a force of nature instead of a feverish selfish little clod of ailments and grievances complaining that the world will not devote itself to making you happy." (George Bernard Shaw)

Time and Deadlines...

There's a fascinating and somewhat sobering idea that most of us need a regular reminder of; that our time is infinitely more valuable than our money. Though on the surface of this you might think this is simply stating the obvious, it is not obvious to the majority of people.

If it was the case people would spend their time more wisely rather than going around with the contention that *there's lots more of it if I need it*. Of course that's the exact opposite of what's true. With financial resources, you're able to extend, replace, add to, borrow, recreate from scratch and so on. With time however there's no opportunity to do anything other

than spend it which is done on a second-by-second basis regardless. Stopping the clock is not an option. As it depletes there's no way of replacing your very own personal allocation of the most valuable resource to any human.

So today, alongside all the other things, I want you to really think about how you can be more effective with your time, particularly with the concepts of *timelines and deadlines.*

The word 'deadline' sounds a bit negative doesn't it? There is a distinct finality about the term which people use regularly in their lives and businesses. Yet when people set goals very often they are deadline-free. (By the way, someone I met told me they have started calling deadlines *lifelines*. Interesting!) Part of the reason for not having a deadline is so not to be confronted with the fact that they've not achieved their objective yet. Yet a goal without a deadline is a

fishing rod without any bait. So from this moment on I want you to be sure of two things when setting your 1-2-3. Firstly, that your goal has a **time deadline** and secondly, it has an **allocation of time** – the timeline, so we know whether you've done your objective justice.

The timeline then is laying out a roadmap for your success so it becomes abundantly clear what you have to do in what order and within what time frame to ultimately meet your final deadline.

An interesting slightly deeper process is to sit in a chair and ensure it's at one end of a long room so that you can see the entire room up to the wall in front of you. I would then ask you to ask yourself a question which is, "If this room represented my life what happens at the brick wall?" For many people they might say 'retirement'; for some they might say 'a time for change'. Whatever your answer, decide how many years this equates to in terms of a timeline. Now look at points between you and the wall which are markers or steps along the way on your time journey. Being able to see in your mind's eye what is ahead of you often makes a massive difference to your steely resolve in wanting to get to your destination in the shortest and most successful way possible.

I often think about this driving along in my car. If there is a large stretch of motorway ahead of me I imagine this to be the journey I'm currently on. I look ahead and see marker points of things along the journey, things I know that need to be achieved no matter what. It's often very inspiring to look down this timeline and to be aware of mini deadlines leading up to the ultimate one: the place at which you'll ideally toast your success.

In doing this timeline exercise today – your mission is to write down what you see, create goal cards if need be and perhaps do this more often from time to time in the future.

Day 23

"Win the hearts and the mind will follow." (Roy H Williams)

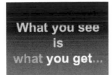

What you see is what you get

It's a well-known fact that most of us spend inordinate amounts of time thinking about what we don't want rather than what we truly desire. Given your mind is a magnet for whatever is in its psyche, if you are thinking about what you don't want you are creating pictures of the very thing that you wish to avoid. The danger of doing this is that by placing the picture in your mind magnet you're actually attracting that very same picture.

I remember having a conversation with a business client who, at the end of their business year, said quite simply that they expected their results to be poor because, "I saw it coming". I couldn't help smiling to myself thinking, "If only you realised what you'd done". This man had set up his year in order to achieve less than adequate results. By thinking that the year was going to be tough and difficult all the pictures in his mind supported what his subconscious assumed to be something he wanted. Had he done it completely the other way around, and seen positive pictures of the way he would have loved the year to unfold, the chances are he would have been successful rather than unsuccessful in that twelve-month period.

So what do you focus on regularly? Do you ever catch yourself spending quality time on worrying and being fearful of things? Because if you do, the chances are things rarely improve; they continue in the same vein. One of the reasons for reading your goal cards every day is to ensure there's a real opportunity to get the right pictures in focus. The bottom line is quite simply this:

The things you focus on always materialise whether they be good or bad. The quality of the pictures is directly linked with the quality and success in your life.

By the way, for most of us, we walk around blissfully unaware that we're being coached by a voice in our head that we ultimately listen to, particularly around decision making.

The voice at times can go completely contrary to our gut instinct and yet since we lack the courage to do the right thing and really listen to ourselves as mentioned before, we go with the flow and align ourselves with the voice.

 If you become more aware of what the voice says, you'll be able to work out whether you are quite a positive or a rather negative individual. One of the challenges in this process is the simple act of denial. I'm amazed how there are some people who declare that they do not have any such voice guiding them and that they are their own person. If only this was the case. We all have this alto ego and we all listen to the voice.

The trick, if it is a trick, is to circumnavigate the voice, particularly when it's being extremely negative and stopping you from moving towards the things that you want to achieve. It's staggering how many parents put their children off from reaching the stars either because their negative beliefs tell them that most good things are impossible or, in a perverse sort of way, since they never achieved greatness in their lives they certainly don't wish their children to do so. A completely selfish attitude yet sadly commonplace in people.

One of the simplest ways of calming your voice is to tell it to shut up. Now I want to be clear that I'm not encouraging schizophrenia! And, I'm sure you know what I mean. Whenever you get put off by doubt, fear and lack of confidence when negative thinking permeates your entire being and you know it's creating a lack of confidence within, try stepping out of it and telling that voice to be quiet and then do the reverse of what it wanted you to do.

So today when you set your 1-2-3, check the quality of the goal, ensure what you're choosing is exciting and worthy of your attention. It's all about mental quality control.

A quick reminder: do ensure your personal diary is up to date and why not for the first time since the start of this journey have a little peek at some of your early entries and ask yourself whether you have in any way changed in your outlook. I do hope as I surmise that you will be pleasantly surprised to notice that a change, however small, has indeed manifested.

Also today I want you to think about a major goal then ask yourself the question, who today could I speak with who would definitely help me get much closer. It may indeed be someone outrageously successful in this area or famous. Now I want you to do one of two things. Call them or write to them by letter. (As opposed to e-mail).

Yes, I am serious. What's the worst that could happen? And if you get a gatekeeper coming back to you, see if you can strike up a relationship with them, and persist in your task.

Day 24

"People can only go to those places that they have already been in their minds." (Roy H Williams)

Controlling your feelings

Welcome to Day 24. Today's helping of success comes in the form of understanding how to control your feelings. Imagine being able to do this at all times – being able to control negative feelings and convert them into positive ones. Yet all of us have it within ourselves to be able to do this. It's just that few of us have been told what to do in practical terms.

The Reverse Spin Technique

Sit in a chair and on this occasion I want you to think of something negative on purpose. Score it out of ten and ideally it should be a high score indicating high negativity. Now what I would like you to do is to decide where the feeling is emanating from. Is it for example in your head? Your neck? Your stomach? (If I remind you that we often talk about our stomach 'turning' this will help the exercise make even more sense.) Let's suppose it's in your neck. Now mime removing this feeling a bit like a grey ball from your neck, taking it out and letting it hang in mid-air in front of you. Notice this grey ball is spinning. Which way is it spinning? Once you've ascertained the direction, spin it in exactly the opposite way as fast as you can. While it's spinning in its new direction, change the colour of the ball to your favourite colour. Okay, how does it feel now? For most people there is a definite improvement in the feeling and if you were to do this regularly you could indeed change a negative feeling into something positive in moments. Very powerful indeed.

Identifying the Mind Windows

Once again sit on a chair and relax. Now point in front of you where you can feel negativity. Let's imagine you pointed down and to your right (for each person this is very different). Keeping your finger pointed in that direction, take your other hand and do the same exercise with pointing to somewhere which feels good. Let's imagine this is up and to your left. (It could be anywhere).

What I'd now like you to do is to tie an imaginary elastic band between your two index fingers and I want you to shape a rubber ball where the good feeling exists and for the rubber ball to be connected to the elastic band. Now pull back on the rubber ball which is a ball of good feelings and let it fly and hurtle towards the other index finger pointing to the bad feeling. Once the imaginary ball hits the bad feeling let it completely encapsulate it with the good positive sensation.

This is all rather a strange idea and yet when done properly will sometimes completely eradicate the negative feeling and replace it with one that will make you smile. Provided there is a change in the feeling from bad to good, repeating this process will normally completely take the negative feeling away, leaving you feeling more motivated and inspired.

Face/body tapping

This technique is one that I learned from a Paul McKenna workshop I attended. It's sometimes called 'temporal tapping'.

Instructions.

- Taking two fingers tap one side of the forehead
- After 8-10 taps do the same under the opposite side of the face – under the eye
- Now to the opposite side of the face again top lip
- Whilst doing the top lip roll eyes from one side to the other x 2
- Go to the other side of the face – bottom chin
- Whilst tapping bottom of chin hum 'happy birthday' followed by counting backwards from 10 to 1.
- Tap shoulder area (clavicle) on other side of body
- Go to under arm other side of body tapping here
- Remain on this side of the body, tap between the third and fourth finger on top of the hand
- Finally, raise the hand like a karate chop gesture – same side of the body and tap the side of the hand.

Now repeat this again.

When you are doing this technique, also known as TFT, or EFT, it's important to check what score you have at the beginning of the process – and then compare it

THE SIXTY DAY SUCCESS BLOG

at the end. Provided you feel there's a difference you can continue doing this technique until your feelings have completely altered for the feeling you want to change.

So today is getting control of your feelings. Try some of these techniques and remember your daily blog entry.

Day 25

"If you worried about falling off the bike, you would never get on." (Lance Armstrong)

Success attainment is like a good diet, the more you do it the more you see results. So here we are in the fourth week and hopefully you've been following this sixty-day diet on a day-by-day basis. If you have been, well done; boy are you doing well. If on the other hand you've taken a little longer to get to this point, remember that there's power in momentum – maybe have the book near your bed to read it in the morning or last thing at night for the next day?

To summarise where you are hopefully:

- You should know what you want, why you want it, when you want it and how you intend to achieve it.
- There should be more order and organisation in your life and a sense of clarity and purpose.
- You should now have embarked upon new habits of personal effectiveness.
- Your view of attaining success should be one which has improved in terms of self-belief and the realisation that success can be attained in small bite-size chunks day by day.
- That a 1-2-3 system is a great tactical way of attaining small regular goals. Remember that few humans set and achieve daily goals, and the fact that you are now doing this truly shoots you forward into the super league of goal achievers.

It's strange how when I talk to people about goals, the majority see goals as something big. Now there's nothing wrong with thinking big unless of course the thought prevents you from taking action. As John F Kennedy once said, "There are costs and risks to a program of action but they are far less than the long-range risks and costs of comfortable inaction". So a further sanity check at this stage and a question I'd like you to ask yourself, "Have I been allowing myself to experience the comfortable nature of inaction in the last twenty four days?" Given that this is a sixty-day journey and that this 'book blog' has been designed for you to take daily steps, it's important for me as your coach to remind you about critical success factors.

Action -vs- Inaction

One of the most obvious which constantly gets overlooked is the nature of inaction versus action. On the surface of it, it may appear that you'd be daft to not know that these two concepts are poles apart. Quite simply one is about doing something and the other is the complete opposite – doing nothing. Yet

people focused on attaining success get really confused sometimes and actually believe they are taking action when they are in fact remaining motionless and in such a state removing any reality around attaining the success they are so desperately seeking.

You'll remember that inaction is a state created by interference, a thought or stream of thoughts which attacks your subconscious like a disease, creating instant paralysis towards the attainment of outcomes. These thoughts may simply be a few negative comments, which are often based on previous experiences in your life, or they may be major barriers that on the surface appear insurmountable. Many people refer to these as problems. Tomorrow we'll look at dealing with these issues.

For today however I'd like you to look back on the last days since day one and identify any agreed actions that have in fact _not been actioned_. Make a list and write down next to each non-action the reason why it hasn't happened yet. Let's hope that this list is a very small one and maybe for some you draw a blank. If you fall in this category, carry on the good work and ensure your daily regime is dealt with and I'll catch you tomorrow.

For the rest who do have things to write on this list, I'd like you to dig deep. Some real honesty would be much appreciated at this stage. Let's imagine on your list one of your actions was to find someone to help you in marketing a new business idea. Next to this action you might have written, "Don't know anyone in marketing". Now what you might want to do is to really think about your excuse, because that's exactly what it is, and imagine for a moment that you were helping someone else in their business and they came up with this very same thing. What would you want to say to them? Would you agree with them, or would you want to *reframe* the challenge in some way. I'm pretty sure it will be the latter and it's now time to challenge yourself. Quite simply if your life was on the line what would you have really done around your marketing action in this example? Get that list written, challenge, reframe and join me for tomorrow's entry.

Day 26

"One of my favourite pastimes is fantasising about future success." (Richard Branson)

I was recently asked by someone whether a book could be read without necessarily attaching it to a project or set of goals. Though I was happy to offer some thoughts to this lady, I had to smile at the same time because isn't this the nature of most self-development books? Sad but true, there are hundreds of thousands of books in the world that offer you quick fixes and *how to do it,* and it's so easy in a state of comfortable inaction to read the content at the same time say to yourself, "yes I must do that one day".

The whole purpose of this collection of blog entries is to get you off your chair, get you looking in the right direction, and help you light the blue touch paper of the fuse that triggers true motivation and passion in your mind that then drives you to wherever you want to go or whatever you want to achieve. Doing is 99% of what success is all about. The final 1% is the outcome, result or conclusion, and provided you did the 99% consistently and continually you will *always achieve what you want.*

Dealing with Problems

Isn't it curious how here in Great Britain we use the 'p' word a lot: problems.

A great many of our cousins in North America however, prefer to call them challenges and so when I ask someone here to change the word problem into challenge, I invariably get a groan in return. The belief that many people have in the UK is that a problem is a problem and changing the word is not going to make any difference whatsoever. I totally disagree. If you think about it, the language we use, whether it be positive or negative has a direct influence on our actions or inactions as the case may be. Have you never been sitting in front of a television advertisement and an image or a word either makes you get up to have whatever it is they're advertising or go out and buy some at the next available opportunity? It might be that you declare that such things would never affect you. I don't believe it. Whether you like it or not television advertising is very powerful indeed and for most of the time the words and pictures are not talking to you, they're talking to your subconscious. I was amazed how quickly my eldest son began recognising brand names and logos from a young age, especially considering what little TV we allowed him to watch.

Why do you think the volume level increases on your TV set during the adverts? The advertisers are already well aware that you're likely to be talking over the adverts so they want to be absolutely sure your subconscious hears every word!

I have to raise my hands and say that I get very irritated when negative words are used unnecessarily. I've even struggled to use the word 'fail' in this book though felt it necessary so that people understand what I'm trying to say.

Let's be clear, this is not about hiding from the truth or pretending that something is good when it is quite the opposite. It's about not jumping to conclusions, not giving up before you've started and not surrendering to what you perceive to be the inevitable when it's anything but.

Let me give you an example: a friend of mine was working on a house project where he'd bought a piece of land and started to convert an old derelict building which stood on it. Halfway through construction I heard he had a major 'problem'. Apparently there was an underground stream going underneath the building which sometimes had little effect on the structure and at other times created dampness at an unprecedented scale. He rang to tell me of his woes and all the language around the issue was dire and extremely negative, "Dean, all that money I've spent has literally gone down the drain. I'm not even sure I can sell this piece of land now because who'd want to have a dwelling on this?"

His focus then turned to suing his surveyor and in fact doing everything but continue with his dream goal. I was shocked, and so was he when he realised what surprised me. The fact that he had given up without a fight, bathed in negative language which was forcing him down this route in the first place. I did manage to  get him to agree to meet up and re-evaluate the situation. We started by reframing his thinking and rewording some of his current beliefs, which by nature of a positive translation did spark a different take on matters entirely. To cut a very long story short, he went away and made it his business to find other experts to advise him and eventually the solution got him back on track in a way he never thought possible.

Now he has this wonderful house in the country with a stream he can actually see in part of the building through glass floorboards. There is no more dampness and his unique home has doubled in value since he bought the land. By making contact with so many other experts he has also unearthed opportunities to develop other properties which he would never have discovered had he not been challenged by his underground stream in the first place.

So have you been challenged on your journey yet? I bet you have... and maybe you should think about how you've dealt with the issues so far.

It could be that some of your challenges have been quite small and you've simply ignored them and for those who have had slightly bigger challenges to deal with, you've made it your job to 'fly over the storm' rather than straight through it.

Over the next couple of days I'd like to give you some more specific tools to deal with the 'P' word, or problems. For today, I'd simply like you to make friends with the idea that challenges are part of the fabric of attaining success and without them true success is well-nigh impossible. After all, without results and challenges the word success would not exist. It only exists because we compare it to an opposite concept and wouldn't it be a boring world if everything we set out to do we instantly achieved.

I like to think of success as a person who hides themselves in the middle of a field of hurdles and obstacles. The majority of people will look into this field and see nothing but 'can't-do' while the true entrepreneur of success keeps sifting through everything in this field until they find the way in and smiling face of success looking back, often perched in a place where people least expect to find it.

There's a Latin phrase to remember:

Ad Astra per aspera

It means: to reach the stars means adversity.

Your challenge today around your 1-2-3 is to pick at least one item which you've previously identified as a so-called problem. Decide to call it a challenge, look into it with new eyes and look for the window of opportunity within. Catch you tomorrow.

Day 27

"The man who has no imagination, has no wings."
(Mohammed Ali)

Here's hoping that you've already had some initial success whatever your project or objectives may be and that you're using not just each day's segment as part of your support structure, but going back in previous days and reminding yourself of earlier tools, techniques and ideas that will ultimately provide you with everything you need to achieve your key objective(s) by Day 60.

Yesterday we were looking at the concept of challenges and how it's important to reframe your thinking in order that you see a challenge as an opportunity, a window or door that opens and offers you an insight you've never seen before. Without that challenge, you would have lived your life in blissful ignorance and comfortable inaction. It was the challenge that made you sit up, take notice and above all take the steps you did.

Today I'd like you to consider some tools and techniques for some of the bigger barriers to success that may or may not appear along the way. Being prepared is always a good policy.

The Top Six Problem Busters

1. Take some sort of Immediate Action

As strange as this may seem and indeed as obvious as it appears, few people are prepared to take any immediate action when faced with a challenge, particularly a serious one. The 'bury one's head in the sand and hope it goes away' mentality is the most popular but that simply creates *inaction*.

So there's a tremendous amount of power in taking a step forward to deal with whatever's confronting you. There will be those who say that sometimes when challenged with something serious one has to reflect in order to make the right decision. The reality is that tor most of us we know what needs to be done and we simply are reluctant to do it.

Taking action can be as simple as making a phone call, asking someone else for their point of view or advice or selecting one of the other Problem Busters that follow.

2. Meeting of minds

Another classic saying is, "A problem shared is a problem halved". True, it almost certainly is. There's something very therapeutic about sharing an issue with someone well placed to assist you in offering good advice. Occasionally it's as simple as finding someone with enough knowledge and experience who can instantly set you on the right path. More often, it's somebody who simply has a point of view that you've not considered before because you've been too close to your challenge. Interesting, isn't it that we are often happy to offer solutions to someone else's challenge and it's only when we own the challenge ourselves that we appear to have difficulty in coming up with solutions.

3. Make it visual

The majority of the world's population are strong visuals. In other words what they see makes a big difference to them. This is particularly the case around challenges where simply hearing a problem in your head like an old broken record is not the same as mapping it out on a piece of paper or flipchart so that not only can you see it clearly but others can come along and offer their advice too. It might just be that the act of creating a diagram also creates a solution at the same time.

4. Role-play the solution

Imagine you're in a play and in this play there's no script. This means you have to ad-lib and make up the lines as you go along. You play the part of someone helping someone else with a problem. The question is, if you intend to be a first-class actor in this performance, are you likely to be able to come up with lines that actually offer a solution? Of course the chances are that you would. If you were to use the same process in a real situation where you were talking through solutions to your so-called problem with someone else, with both of you in a 'stepping into the future' mode the chances are some amazing ideas would emerge.

5. Beyond the Box

One of the most common expressions these days, particularly in businesses, is: 'think outside the box'. I always smile when I ask people who use this expression what it actually means. These days, very few people can actually give me the answer.

It originates from a classic puzzle in the 70s/80s consisting of nine dots where you're requested to join all nine dots with four straight lines without going through any line twice or your pen leaving the paper. The only way to achieve success is in fact to draw beyond the dots which make a square shape. Hence the expression, *think outside the box.*

In other words, do yourself a big favour and really think of the less obvious in terms of dealing with your challenge.

When coaching businesses with formidable challenges, the key players in the organisation have always managed to come up with two lists of dealing with the way forward. A list of traditional solutions and often a much longer list of so-called bizarre even completely over-the-top ideas.

I recall the company who were having terrific problems hitting sales targets and someone on the board thought he'd make a joke. He said tongue in cheek, "Let's sack the sales team and sell everything on line". After the laughter died down, the entire board started to look at each other intrigued. Sad for the sales guys, yet the company is still thriving today and their sales have quadrupled as a result.

6. Getting things into Perspective

One Problem Buster that's nearly always overlooked is to get things into a clearly defined perspective. Most challenges are nearly always overstated or exaggerated and it's about perspective.

Where one individual sees it as a major challenge, another sees it as 'a walk in the park'. If you're dealing with your difficulty yourself, scale it down by first of all comparing it with other things that could have happened and haven't. Comparison chunks it down to size and makes it instantly less oppressive.

The other thing you can do is to acknowledge all the good things that are currently going well for you. Take a piece of paper and draw a line down the centre of the page. In the left-hand column write down the challenge or challenges and in the right-hand column write down everything that's an advantage or going well in life that's you're grateful for. If you really go for it on the advantages just the simple act of doing this will make you feel that something inside you has shifted and you have a different appreciation for a suddenly scaled-down problem list that you feel more confident of dealing with.

Day 28

"The caterpillar knows she is designed for something greater." (Jim Rohn)

When I was growing up I remember creativity being mentioned at school. It was linked to great inventors like Alexander Fleming who discovered penicillin and Alexander Graham Bell who invented the telephone. The downside of receiving information in this way is that as a child you think that being creative is something that's allocated to the genius few and is not something connected to the likes of the general population at large. Nothing could be further from the truth. Take a look at this excerpt from a story in 2007:

Tony Cicoria was forty-two, and a fit former college football player who had become a highly skilled orthopedic surgeon near New York.

He was at a lakeside pavilion for a family gathering one afternoon when he noticed that it looked like rain was imminent.

Before the advent of mobiles, he went to a payphone to make a call. Then all hell broke loose. The distant

 thunder was suddenly tapping him on the shoulder and before he knew it, he got struck down by lightning.

This was no ordinary lightning strike. Tony remembers the force actually coming down the phone line and hitting him squarely in the face.

He also recalls: "I was flying forwards. Bewildered. I looked around. I saw my own body on the ground. I said to myself, 'I'm dead.' I saw people converging on the body. I saw a woman — she had been standing waiting to use the phone right behind me — position herself over my body, give it CPR. . . . I floated up the stairs — my consciousness came with me. I saw my kids, had the realization that they would be okay. Then I was surrounded by a bluish-white light . . . an enormous feeling of well-being and peace. The highest and lowest points of my life raced by me. No emotion associated with these ... pure thought, pure ecstasy. I had the perception of accelerating, being drawn up .. there was speed and direction. Then, as I was saying to myself, 'This is the most glorious feeling I have ever had' — SLAM! I was back."

The doctor knew he was back in his body because now he could feel the pain running through it. He was fortunate in having had an angel of mercy in the form of a critical care nurse who brought him back.

It's interesting that he also felt unsure if he wanted to come back! The feeling of his NDE or near death experience was that of 'ecstasy' and a trip to a cardiologist confirmed no heart damage. He was going to be okay. Furthermore, tests on his brain also revealed nothing amiss. He was in the clear.

Soon he was back in the operating theatres but apart from minor memory problems which soon vanished he was deemed as fully recovered.

What now followed was quite extraordinary to say the least.

Tony started to have a real desire to listen to piano music. Okay he had some schoolboy type lessons when he was young but to this point had no passion or desire to listen to the piano. Something immense had emerged almost from nowhere. Along these lines he also started buying music, namely Vladimir

Ashkenazy and Chopin, and with the listening then came the need to play them. By an interesting turn of events he managed to get his hands on an upright piano never having had a piano before – and started to play. What really helped, was starting to hear the music in his mind as he attempted to play it. These two aspects began to fuse together. He found himself teaching himself. One must remember we're talking about an orthopedic surgeon here with no previous bent for piano music.

Following this came composing. He felt a very powerful presence from within – giving him music to write down and reproduce. At times he described himself as being overwhelmed. From deep down inside, he was being inspired.

"It's like a frequency, a radio band. If I open myself up, it comes. I want to say, 'It comes from heaven,' as Mozart said." His music is ceaseless. "It never runs dry," he continued. "If anything, I have to turn it off."

Quite simply, he became a man possessed.

Like a midlife crisis, his notions were moving away from medicine and firmly towards music. In fact his thoughts were shaping along the lines of this being his raison d'être in life, not surgery.

Most recently he put on a sell-out concert in New York and received very impressive reviews from the classical music world. Since the lightning strike, he's received a new appreciation of life on a variety of levels. His left-brain science has given way to right-brain art, something he would have sworn was not inside him before the unusual accident.

Of course the sceptics will say that this is some sort of mental aberration and is not natural at all. This would be a fair comment if it was the first time it had ever happened, yet this kind of situation has happened many times before with a whole variety of people. For example, people having head injuries and waking up speaking a foreign language and having to re-learn your mother tongue.

The human mind continues to be the most amazing powerhouse of infinite possibility. You have one yourself, and I'm delighted to inform you that you were born with all the skills that humans possess at birth. This would mean, for example, that you are indeed an opera singer. And I can hear you saying to yourself, "But I'm not..." The fact that you choose not to use your in-built skill because you have no desire to sing is of course another issue again. There is certainly no doubt in my mind that if you suddenly became passionate about wanting to sing opera the potential is there waiting to be stimulated .

So today:

- Who would you really like to be?
- What would you really like to do?
- How long are you going to wait before you realise the sea of potential you harbour?

Day 29

"A common problem with entrepreneurs is that they spend most of their time defending what they know rather than learning what they don't know." (Michael Gerber)

Today we are staying with creativity a little longer.

Let's furnish you with some ways to really use your in-built creative potential. Starting with some basics, it's widely acknowledged that the right side of the human brain deals with more creative matters than the left side. I'm aware that not every physiologist and psychologist shares this point of view, though at the time of writing this book, most do. In effect, I'm going to suggest that it probably doesn't matter at all. If you wish to think and be creative your brain will know what to do. It's having the confidence to allow it to do so on your behalf.

Let's try something.

Sit comfortably in a chair and put your feet on the floor with your hands on your lap. Relax and look straight ahead. Now allow your eyes to roll up and to your left. Try and memorise the feeling associated with you doing this while you think of a goal you wish to achieve in the next twelve months. When you've done this sufficiently I'd like you now to look up and to your right and think of the same goal. You may then wish to switch from left to right and compare the feelings attached to these two eye movements. I'd like you to determine which way you prefer to look which makes you feel more capable of achieving your success.

Whichever way it is, this is the way to always look if you desire the most creative thoughts. Creativity also comes with colour and the use of all your senses. See it, voice it and feel how it feels. Given we're all creatures of habit and have a preference for the visual, auditory or feeling and emotional way of inputting information to our brain, it's very easy to get stuck in one of these areas, ignoring the other two. Additional creativity always comes when you include all your five senses if possible.

One of my favourite episodes on the Channel 4 hit TV series, *Faking It* where individuals are challenged in terms of acquiring new skills for a profession far removed from their current one in just thirty days.

In this episode a painter and decorator, who acknowledged his creative flair didn't go much beyond lining up the wallpaper correctly and ensuring the paint was coated evenly on all surfaces, found himself learning how to create modern art works which he subsequently sold after thirty days for

THE SIXTY DAY SUCCESS BLOG

thousands of pounds. The confidence he gleaned from being coached by successful artists and art experts kick-started his inner creativity in ways he never thought possible. I'm glad to say he was not struck by lightning nor did he have to endure some awful accident for the true artist within to emerge and take centre stage.

Day 30

"It's never what you do in life, it's always how you do it."
(Keith Cunningham)

Big Challenge Day

Today's a really big day because it's time to see what you're made of! There's an interesting little ploy that I sometimes use on my coaching clients where I ask them to hold their breath for as long as they are able  and to raise their hand when they need to take another breath. At this point I will tell them how long they've managed to go for and then ask them to have another go in the same time frame yet to go all out to beat their record.

Isn't it curious that every time I do this without fail the individual will beat their score the second time. In fact, I've never had anyone not beat their score.

There is however once piece of information I must reveal to you now. Let's imagine that I was sitting with you and asked you to hold your breath and I noted that you managed to do it for twenty-five seconds. My ploy is to exaggerate the amount of time and perhaps add an additional ten seconds and tell you that you had managed to hold your breath for thirty-five seconds.

The second time you go through this process I actually give you my watch so that you can look at the time as you hold your breath. I think you can see what happens. Because you believe that you did thirty-five seconds and you're eager to break your record, the chances are you'll go to forty, forty-five seconds or more... only to be told at the end that you were misinformed and in fact your first score was a mere twenty-five seconds.

The learning here is quite profound. There must be an inner voice that tells people to stop and take another breath first time round, even though you had the ability to go longer. On the second occasion you have something to look at and aim for; it gives you a way of beating your believed target.

When this was first done to me I was staggered. It hit me like an express train; the fact that I have so much more to give yet invariably I'm allowing limiting beliefs to overtake me or simply *to take me over!* Think about this while I take you back to your big challenge today.

The challenge is to look back at the Problem Buster tools and your creativity techniques and using as much of it as possible work out how you can make your current objectives bigger, bolder, more exciting and more successful today.

One of the most inspirational questions I always think about from time to time in my own life is:

"What great thing could I achieve today if I knew I could not possibly fail...?"

All I'm asking of you here is to let go of the shackles holding you back and with nothing to lose, step outside your comfort circle. It may also be an idea to set a time limit around this so that there's a sense of urgency.

When you've gone through this process and have a way forward written down, I'd like you to go on and create a roadmap or a list of next steps which have practical straightforward and easy-to-implement actions attached. Then, guess what? Take full and positive action and really push the boat out.

All of the individuals I've ever known or read about who have 'rags to riches' stories to tell are invariably very straightforward people. They rarely had a quality education or much money when they first started out. The thing that they all do have in common however is in-built self-motivation and a real passion and vision in what they are striving for.

Day 31

"You cannot take the mild approach to weeds in your mental garden. You have got to hate weeds enough to kill them. Weeds are not something you handle, weeds are something you devastate." (Jim Rohn)

Let's look at a set of Success Laws, universal laws if you like, that have been around since time began. You may have already heard of this kind of thing before and I'm going to ask you to set aside any previous associations or beliefs.

We're all aware of physical laws such as the Law of Gravity. Laws which now can be explained scientifically yet once were a complete mystery. I'd like to suggest that the laws we're going to look at for the next few days could all be explained scientifically and yet in our history of understanding we're still not quite there yet.

Before we begin with the first law, let me remind you that you should be planning to do a quick review tomorrow of where you are with your current project, goals and ambitions and also look back at some of your previous diary entries, particularly those positive ones that will spur you on to the finishing line. Over the next few days we'll be exploring Six Universal Laws I wish to bring to your attention.

Let's start with one you'd never expect in this book!

The Law of Failure

Now here's a surprise... perhaps this is the last law you'd ever think we'd be discussing in a journey of success. Yet the law of failure is all around us. Like all universal laws it's practised regularly and believed in wholeheartedly. And so it's a law that challenges and defies people if only they'd see it in this context. Given that most humans are more afraid of succeeding than they are of failing, we can already see how entrenched the Law of Failure is within our culture and very being. If the Law of Failure were to be defined it could be defined as follows:

The Law of Failure exists to be challenged by success seekers. If we are content to accept second best and do nothing to elevate our thinking, the law keeps us a captive in a mental prison of our own making.

The great thing about this law is that it has to exist for us to be able to measure success. If there was no failure there could be no success surely? Therefore it's a worthy law to be aware of, provided you know how to deal with it, and it's a bit like electricity which can save a life or indeed take a life. Examples of failures who did just that – people who worked through it and were ultimately hailed and revered as absolute success stories – include:

- Abraham Lincoln – bankrupt three times, went on to become President of the United States
- Mahatma Gandhi – worked his way through the law to create an independent India
- Thomas Edison – went through volumes of failure (or was it simply results?) and ended up inventing the electric light bulb
- T J Watson – plummeted from his high-ranking position in one company and moved on to creating his own – IBM
- Donald Trump – made a fortune, lost a fortune – made an even bigger fortune.

If there was no *reaction* to the inertia created by failure, the success would have been overlooked or simply dismissed as possible.

Though failure needs to be given a wide berth, whenever the law grabs you from nowhere and makes you topple, you need to stand up again, and keep doing this persistently until you're back on top. A further purpose of the law is to teach you lessons. Lessons that you learn from. Lessons that give you leverage.

It's a shame that for many of us our failing is to not fully embrace the aftermath of any failure and the hunting out of the lesson it provides for us to become stronger in our continued quest for what we want. Instead by not fully engaging with this law, we are in danger of running into the same lesson time and time and time again. If we're not careful, we end up making the law a habit or way of doing something when it was only intended to be there for reflective creation reasons.

Today I'd like you to grab a clean sheet of paper and take three or four minutes to download as many failures that you can think of in your lifetime. If you're immediately thinking that the list is endless, then simply choose your top six or top ten. Then go through the list again and write next to each item what the lesson to learn was. I bet you've never done this before. Time to change that.

Whilst doing this you might like to consider whether the lesson has recurred or in fact you learned sufficiently from it to move. Once you really get a handle on the Law of Failure and you are fully aware of its purpose then it's time to move on.

Dealing with the Law of Failure

Should the Law of Failure present itself to you, know it's for a reason. It's time to learn something – so embrace it. Then seek out what you need to learn and move on.

The more time you spend commiserating with yourself and licking your wounds, the bigger the danger of being unable to break free. I'm not aware of any human being, regardless of how wealthy or successful they appear to be, who doesn't have to deal with the law of failure from time to time. Being financially secure doesn't always mean you can be spiritually secure. Where money can assist you in a whole variety of so-called problems, it's rarely been the panacea to the challenges in life around relationships. And we know some of the wealthiest people on the planet still go to their doctors with stress, mental exhaustion and depression. And finally with this law I always replace the word 'failure' in my own life with 'result'!

Day 32

"Argue for your limitations, and sure enough they are yours." (Richard Bach)

So today it's time to review the Law of Knowledge.

The Law of Knowledge

At a very early age I remember my father saying to me that 'knowledge is power'. There is undoubtedly some truth in this yet knowledge on its own without anything applied to it is unlikely to be of much help to anyone.

If the Law of Knowledge had an explanatory definition attached to it, it might be:

The law of knowledge states that if we increase the amount of information we need to know about the goals we've set out to achieve, we are likely to stumble upon quicker and more effective ways to create our outcomes.

Today we live in an amazing *infomedia* age. We are on the verge of becoming *infomaniacs* too. So as long as we deal with information in the best way, we are going to be in the best position to benefit.

The Internet provides us with the knowledge on just about anything. It's so easy to tap into and often takes a few seconds to get to the heart of what we need to know. Despite this, people still fail to fully utilise the free knowledge, and all it can bring. In order to get to the final destination it's important that you make yourself knowledge hungry around the things you wish to achieve. Are you fully up to date with what's going on in the world around **your subject or goal?**

Knowledge or content is often deemed as 'king'. Comedian Bob Monkhouse carried all his jokes handwritten in a book which ended up being stolen. The bottom fell out of his world.

He was painfully aware that the originality of a lot of his humour came from jokes he'd heard or dreamed up himself which he committed to paper. Without that knowledge he was only a fraction of the comedian he truly was. Content was definitely 'king' in this situation. And If you think about it, some of the top movies in the world started as an idea in someone's head, which they eventually got paid for in millions of dollars.

The benefit of understanding the importance of the Law of Knowledge is that knowing more takes us from a corridor with two or three doors into a football stadium of corridors with hundreds upon thousands of doors. Each door is an opportunity and each opportunity has the possibility of limitless outcomes. So we often limit ourselves by playing in a small corridor

THE SIXTY DAY SUCCESS BLOG

rather than seek out the vast expanse of endless possibility that's more often than not just waiting for us around the corner.

My question to you today is whether you have been limiting yourself on knowledge assuming you know enough already. The Law of Knowledge indicates that we can never know enough about anything, whoever we might be. When we stop learning, we put the lid on materialising our desired future. Thirst for knowing more in a never-ending spiral that takes us higher and higher in our ideals is what the law of knowledge is there to remind us about.

Your task is to spend one hour on the Internet, or book store or media store. Download, buy or borrow some more knowledge – as profound as you dare on your goal(s). Do it today. Do it now...

Day 33

"There are two ways to live your life. One is as though nothing is a miracle, the other is as though everything is a miracle." (Albert Einstein)

The Law of Cause and Effect

Much has been written about this well-known law for centuries. There are various definitions and ways to explain the law, and perhaps the easiest way to put it in words could be:

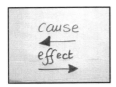

Every action has an equal and rebounding action.

Some people call this 'The Boomerang Principle'. In recent years discussing this with some members of the scientific community, they could not understand how this could possibly work, and were quite amused at the idea of this being any kind of law.

By the way, this same scientific community once postulated that the world was flat.

I suggest the best way to get in touch with this law is your gut feeling. Have you ever been in a situation where you've done something good for somebody else and not long after someone independent of that person has come back and done something good for you? It's certainly true in business. The more action you take in terms of marketing messages, calls to prospective customers, PR and so on – the more likely you are to have a business which is active, buzzing and ultimately thriving. Take no action and guess what, nothing happens.

This whole sixty-day success blog is about taking action on a daily basis and hopefully as each day passes you are doing just that, as well as learning new ideas and concepts to support your continuous focus.

In the East the law of cause and effect is known as 'karma'. You may be aware that Beatle John Lennon wrote a song about the subject in his song *Instant Karma*. Business karma then is very much about how you deal with your customers and the products and services you sell and market. Isn't it also true that the businesses that have a couldn't-care-less attitude about their customers soon succumb to a massive loss of customers and the inevitability of crashing and burning? In whatever project you are applying these principles to, have you carefully crafted a customer proposition where you're absolutely certain your customer will not just be satisfied but highly delighted, indeed over the moon with your offering?

Think about this. How many businesses or suppliers of goods and services that you patronise also deliver amazing, if not thoroughly awesome, customer service? Most businesses will agree with this concept and very few actually deliver it. As an entrepreneur yourself, you have the power to make this happen in your organisation, even if you are a one-man band.

If you want to succeed in an online business, the standard of excellent service is likely to massively impact your results.

Leaving Eastern philosophies aside now, let's look at the Law of Cause and Effect in a cold hard light. In its most simple form it's suggesting that whatever you put out will swing back in your direction. Let's look at the logic behind it. It makes perfect sense. If all the personal development books on our planet were to be analysed for the most popular and indeed the number one tool for success, it would almost certainly

be *take action*. Here then is an action-centred law. It can do no harm to think about it in everything you do, and I suggest being aware of it will bring what you want to you *much faster*.

You may also like to consider the fact that the law rarely works if you attempt to manipulate it. For example, if you're taking action only because you are setting up something to come back to you, then you miss the point. It's like going to a friend's house and going overboard to help them redecorate it whilst making hints that your own place could do with some refurbishing too. It's most unlikely that they're going to instantly respond and visit you the next day. The other thing to bear in mind is the time interval between cause and effect can be great, and your return doesn't necessarily happen instantly.

Pay it Forward?

Imagine parking your car on a parking meter and later on realising that the time has expired. Let's also imagine that it's in a very busy area in a large city where the chances of the matter going unnoticed are practically zero.

Now see yourself arriving back at your vehicle and sure enough there is something under one of the windscreen wipers. Your heart melts as you walk over to it and take the paper off the car to read it. Now how would you feel about seeing this?

I COULDN'T HELP NOTICING THAT YOUR TIME HAD EXPIRED AND THE FACT A PARKING WARDEN WAS HEADING RIGHT IN THE DIRECTION OF YOUR VEHICLE. I MANAGED TO PUT SOME MORE MONEY IN FOR YOU AND I HOPE YOU'VE BEEN ABLE TO GET BACK IN TIME.

– A FRIEND.

Wow! What would be running through your mind right now?

I've also known situations where someone reached into their pocket and discovered a £50 note. They had gone to a restaurant and hung up their jacket only to find this note had been pushed into it at some point during their meal. This is a kind of reverse form of stealing isn't it? Though I'm not suggesting that you rush out today and do either of these things, I would like you to consider what you could do for somebody – preferably a stranger where you remain completely incognito. Making a real difference to another human being.

I firmly believe it's a great habit to create which will not just be satisfying but will come back to you in all sorts of ways in the future. Of course the idea is not to do it purely to see what you can get out of it, and before you allow that little voice in your head to say, "I have no idea what I could do", go for a stroll today with the thought of doing some good in your mind and I promise you you'll find an opportunity.

I was walking through a busy city recently and a Big Issue salesperson came straight up to me wanting to sell me a magazine. I placed my hand in my pocket and pulled out a £20 note. The guy initially looked a little peeved, given that he probably didn't have the change, but as I took the magazine from him I said with a smile, "Keep the change". I wish I had a camera to record the amazing reaction which made his day and guess what, made mine.

Today think of a totally unselfish act to give to another human being and action it. Surprise yourself in what you decide to do. And remember it can be a simple phone call.

Then record the outcome in your blog. Enjoy!

Day 34

"In the long run, the race belongs not merely to the swift, but to the farseeing, to those who anticipate change."
(Lykes Lines)

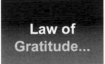

The Law of Gratitude

Surprisingly we take so much for granted. Often we're not aware that there are people, influences and forces behind many of the things that we like, love and want.

If someone is kind enough to take you for a meal it would normally be customary for you to say thank you at the end. Imagine not doing this and how bad you might feel as a result. Isn't it also extraordinary that here in the UK only about 60% of all drivers thank other drivers for their courtesy. Does this mean that the 40% are just plain rude or is there something else going on here?

 Too many of us suffer from an only too common complaint called 'gratitude blindness'. Good things happen to us through events, circumstances or other people and on too many occasions we simply fail to respond with any form of gratitude.

 ### Hot tip #1

Imagine you have a diary where, on a day-by-day basis, you write down all the good things that happened to you that particular day and what you're really grateful about. What you write doesn't have to be a major entry yet each item you include you are genuinely grateful for. If you were to do this exercise you would find that over a relatively short period of time you actually start to feel better about your life! What you're doing is focusing on what's good about things rather than – what most people do

– target their thinking around what isn't working and what's lacking in their lives. The Gratitude Diary gets you constantly focusing on what's possible and will guide you better to greater achievements.

Your task today is to add an additional piece to your daily blog each and every day from today. What you're grateful for…today.

Hot tip #2

Time to draw a mind map or to simply sketch out on a large sheet of paper all the greatest moments in your life. When did you last do this I wonder? I bet you anything you like you've never done it, and if you have, some while ago. So go back in time as far back as you can remember and start putting down all those best moments on the single sheet in front of you. Find photographs to support the evidence!

I have to say it's going to be a little sad if you're looking at this sheet of paper thinking, "I can't think of anything". What you write doesn't have to be completely mind-boggling just things that stick in your mind as golden or magical in your life. Do this, and do it now before reading on.

Okay, take a good long look at everything you've written down and the photos you've unearthed and as your eyes register each event and memory, I want you to linger and savour the moments you're pondering upon. As you do this how are you feeling? What are you thinking? What is this process making you now want to do as a result?

You may wish to consider keeping this sheet somewhere accessible for daily reference. Spend a few moments every day remembering what you've achieved, either directly or indirectly and how important it is to you to remember these feelings and your need to experience more of the same in the future.

Why don't you spend the rest of the day celebrating your past successes as you prepare for your future ones? You did it before; you can do it again, and again ....and keep doing it.

In your daily routines always consider the Law of Gratitude. This law states:

Be grateful for the things today and this gratitude sets up more things to be grateful for tomorrow.

Day 35

"We see best what we are supposed to see. We see poorly or not at all that data that does not fit our paradigm." (Joel Barker)

The Law of Interaction

One of the most amazing things that plagues small businesses or people with a great idea to sell is not that they fail to offer a reasonable proposition, but that no one knows about them in the first place. They remain some of the world's best kept secrets. You may wish to liken it to the success of eBay. All those items for sale were still available to customers before eBay came along. The difference now is the world has access to view the millions of goods on offer, creating an interactive space to transact business 24 hours of the day.

With this in mind let's look at the next law, the Law of Interaction. If this law was to have a log line I'd describe it as:

When your action is supported by the actions of other people, this new state of interactivity invariably generates ideas, opportunities and wealth.

Whether you are starting a business, making a movie, writing a book or making a change in the world in some other way, interaction with other humans – either personally or through technology – will always make a massive difference. Attempting to achieve something in a goldfish bowl or on your own may still get you there, but boy is it likely to be a long hard road...

There's a whole range of ways you can interact with other people. Here are some of them:

• Websites and the Internet	• Photography and visual arts
• Writing articles for magazines	• Creating podcasts
• Reading magazine articles and writing to the author	• On stage as a guest speaker
• Telephone and texts	• Through your very own creative news stories
• Directories and mailing lists	• Through the databases of other people
• Advertising	• Creating your own MP3 recording, video clip or DVD
• Marketing campaigns	• Breakfast clubs
• Television, radio and other media	• Business launches
• Creating a message through a movie	• Business lunches
• Street interviews, campaigns and rallies	• Official presentations

Today I want you to study the list of possibilities and see how many avenues could or should apply to your goal(s). Then work out how you can tap into that interaction. Tomorrow we'll explore some of these in more detail.

Day 36

"The real voyage of discovery consists not in seeking new lands but in seeing with new eyes." (Marcel Proust)

Let's look at some of the ways to get busy with other people.

Breakfast Clubs

In the last ten years the idea of attending a breakfast club has become very fashionable in the small business community. The real way to create leverage here would be to create your own as it's normally the policy that everyone who attends is the only one representing their profession or business interest.

This idea is well within line with the Law of Interaction. To be successful in your project it's important to interact ideally with the right people who may help you. I use the word 'ideally' because often it's not a simple or straightforward matter to know what your ideal catchment market is. In embarking on any journey, discovery can only come from exploration. Some of the greatest gems that will help you in your quest that you've yet to discover will emerge from the networking you've yet to do with others.

Isn't it interesting how we can always solve other people's problems and have such great difficulty with our own? This is one of the things that the Law of Interaction helps with significantly. Having others look at what you're doing in a more detached way without the emotion and spin you place on it yourself. Interaction creates a sounding board allowing you to have your own in-built quality assurance system. Also it's much easier to edit than to conceive. Running your ideas past other people will easily allow them the opportunity to augment and enhance the basics that you've already come up with.

Today define what and how you will action the ideas of interaction. If you're writing a book, find an agent or publisher today, if you're planning to cruise the world, pinpoint the right travel agent or method of travel, if you're starting a business, find an adviser or accountant who can help you get things moving. I think you've probably got the idea. As I have mentioned already. Time flies. There's nothing like *doing it now*.

Day 37

"You must be the change you wish to see in the world."
(Australian Aboriginals)

The Law of Attraction

We looked at this earlier.

This law has been around a long time and has hit the headlines in the last couple of years through Rhonda Byrne's momentous project 'The Secret', that by now you will have already seen.

The Law of Attraction, like all of these laws, could be expressed in a number of ways. I would like to suggest the definition could be:

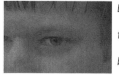

Every thought in your head has a magnetic quality. If the thoughts are positive you'll attract positive things but if the thoughts are negative you will sadly attract the same. Choose the quality of your thoughts and receive in return a quality life.

I have to smile when I talk to people about exploring this law because very often the response is, "Yes I heard about this. What you think is what you get". And then in the same conversation they'll say things like, "Do you know I'm having such a bad year so far. What can you do?" When I refer them back to the Law of Attraction they just shrug their shoulders as if what's that got to do with it?

Hot tip #1

If you're thinking regular positive thoughts and wondering why they are not materialising, you might like to purposely add a small negative in the thought!

Although this sounds contrary to what I've said above, it actually makes perfect sense. The mind will then focus on the negative whilst it allows the bigger positive thought to slip into your subconscious. Here's a silly example but one that really explains how this all works.

Imagine you want to spend a small fortune on a really special meal at a top London hotel. You also want someone special to invite you to the meal in the first place. Your regular thought then would be arriving at this luxury location and walking into a plush restaurant with the person you wish to have the meal with. So far so good. But now let's put in a little negative. How about sitting at the table and enjoying the environment whilst realising that you've achieved your dream and the waiter spills some wine he's pouring on the crisp white tablecloth. This means the entire tablecloth has to be changed which is a really annoying inconvenience on this special occasion. Now if you think of the same thought every day your mind will make heavy weather of the wine spillage, yet it's already placed you in the restaurant with the person you want to be with and in a virtual sense has already made your dream come true. It's because you're allowing yourself to think about a negative thought that there are no more other negative thoughts queuing up for your attention. On the other hand, thinking a positive thought with the absence of any negativity will allow the back door of your thought process to open and little small negatives creep in such as, "But he/she would never invite me to the meal and I'd never be able to spend that kind of money for a meal" and so on.

I remember meeting a businessman some years ago who worked in the software industry. When I visited his offices, I was a little startled to see his face alongside the other faces of some top software gurus in the world. The article was from a well-known magazine on the subject of leaders in software development. When I looked closely I realised that he had substituted his photograph for one of the others in the article which made him look as one of the world's top gurus! He smiled at me and explained that this was not some deliberate attempt to mislead people, simply a little game he was playing to improve his self-image in his own mind. A few months later he was approached by the very same magazine as he had been put forward as a candidate for an awards competition.

It was the 'newcomer to business' competition where different businesses were entering candidates for the prize 'best newcomer'.

Though he never actually won the award, the write-up in the magazine did his business no end of good. Now you may see this as a pure coincidence that the magazine he was playing around with was also the magazine that contacted him out of the blue, yet as far as I'm concerned it's just another example of the Law of Attraction and how powerful it can be.

It's a shame he had some doubts which prevented him winning the award as well. Could it be that life is set up in such a way that whatever you want to have, whoever you want to be and whatever you want to do is merely a question away and that question, "May I have it?" simply requires a way of holding it in your mind regularly and reflecting upon it as if you've already got it.

The reason why this law is probably more important than all the other laws put together is that it's going on day by day, hour by hour, moment by moment. With practice and some foresight you can adapt the law to suit your every need as a human being.

Even in one of the oldest books in the world, the Bible states, "Ask and ye shall receive".

Today I want you to do the following:

Ensure you have 30 index cards with photos and statements, or create a PowerPoint style presentation of the same on your computer preferably with some inspirational music.

If you have time, go on to **youtube.com** and type in words like **inspiration for success, achieving success** and so on. There are hundreds of clips to view, some exceptional, others not that good, but I am sure you'll find a couple that will definitely create a strong mental state to assist you to use the Law of Attraction. Enjoy, and catch you tomorrow.

Day 38

"You cannot discover new oceans unless you have the courage to lose sight of the shore." (Sir Francis Drake)

Had a BFO recently?

Today we're going to look at the person sitting next to you! Just imagine that currently there's somebody wholly invisible sitting at your right elbow. This individual has been attempting to tell you something since the day you were born. Unfortunately, because

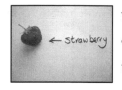

you're not aware of this invisible helper, you're continually and consistently looking ahead and in fact every other direction save where this person is seated, albeit unseen to the naked eye.

What I'm referring to is the source of a BFO and BFO stands for: *A Blinding Flash of the Obvious.*

One example of a BFO relates to French Connection UK Limited. This was a brand that wasn't doing so well until someone realised that a shortened version of their name would certainly grab people's attention. Of course they also realised that given they were marketing to the younger generation not only would the abbreviation be noticed it would probably draw in the rebellious nature of the young four-letter word crowd. This is when the brand FCUK or French Connection UK – *really took off.*

For many a BFO or blinding flash of the obvious is simply getting in touch with their gut feelings. What I come across constantly time and time again is how people are guided by their logical mind and the logic of the situation and completely ignore their gut instinct which is probably more often right than wrong.

Today's task: brainstorm what BFOs you're missing right now that can rocket you towards your dreams, but cannot see because it's so close to you – probably staring you in the face!

A well-known UK retailer, C&A are no longer trading in the UK, though they still have stores in Europe. In fact even though they no longer sell fashionable clothes, the company is very healthy indeed. You see, they had a BFO. They realised that renting their premises out to companies like Next, H&M and Gap was far more profitable to them. So that's what they did, and have done extremely well as a result.

What's your top BFO?

If you have no idea, I bet a few of your close friends will spell it out for you.

Day 39

"An empowered organisation is one in which individuals have the knowledge, skill, desire and opportunity to personally succeed in a way that leads to collective organisational success." (Stephen Covey)

Movies!

Have you ever sat down and listed your top ten favourite movies of all time? Number your top ten on some paper not necessarily in any order, just list those top movies that come into your head; the ones you've most enjoyed seeing.

Although this may appear to be quite frivolous there are various things you can get out of doing this.

First and most obvious thing is to present the list to somebody else, maybe a friend or colleague, and ask them to give their view on your movie list. You'll probably find that by looking at your list they can offer you an insight into the sort of person you are. For example, are you too steeped in a world of fantasy? Or is it more that you like logical movies with a beginning, middle and end?

The second thing to do with your list is to look at those movies which had a strong emotional element. Of course you may argue that any good movie should grab your emotions and there are some movies which are certainly more powerful in this sense than others. Ideally you should then watch those movies that offer you that emotional edge and notice the effect they have on you. The purpose of this exercise is for you to realise that emotion is a strong personal motivator which can of course be positive or negative.

Clearly, it is those movies that offer you a positive punch that you should watch more regularly and use the feelings to drive your goals and ambitions. A similar exercise can be done with your top ten pieces of music of all time – as you will appreciate music is also a way of becoming highly positively charged, given that the medium is so emotive.

So my question for you to consider today is: *are you ruled by your heart or your head?*

Write down a list of all the things that currently your heart or gut is telling you to do. This may be directly or indirectly connected with your goal(s) list.

Now turn the paper over and write down all the logical and sensible things your brain is telling you that you should be doing.

Make a comparison by flitting from the heart list to the head list and ask yourself:

1. Which list is more inspiring?
2. Which is/are you leaning more towards on this journey?
3. Should you make any course corrections today?

Day 40

"It's kind of fun to do the impossible." (Walt Disney)

Buy you... Lunch?

Buy you Lunch?

I bet that there are many people you know as existing friends or contacts through friends of friends. Of this list of people there is a high probability that there are individuals who could help you in all sorts of ways to be more successful. Your challenge today is to think about who you know – directly or indirectly – who you could call up and invite to lunch.

 This should be somebody who could possibly assist you with your journey to success from their knowledge or indeed people that they know further down the line. Engaging with people socially is always a good way to create a relationship and sometimes it's good to take the plunge and meet up with someone who you know of but perhaps have never really met properly. Your choice of individual will largely depend on who you know coupled with your current goals and ambitions. If you want to write that novel it might be someone who knows a literary agent or you wish to go on an expedition then you may wish to connect with somebody who has explorer connections or contacts in the world of sports.

You may also find that if you made it a habit to invite someone to lunch every three months, after a year when you reflect on the four people you've met in this way, it is most unlikely that nothing new has been discovered or gained from meeting up with sometimes complete strangers.

Day 41

"As man sees, so he does." (William Blake)

Books, CDs and DVDs

Apart from this book, what other books and recordings have you bought and are therefore on your list to review that relate to success and achievement?

Over the years I've read many books on personal development and I've always noticed that the more often I've read such material the greater is my ambition, the better my creativity works and as a result I end up achieving so much more. In most good book stores today there is a growing area of books and recorded materials on personal development. Make it a habit to see what else is available and always have a book that you've yet to read in your

car, bag or briefcase so that you never waste precious minutes if the situation presents itself to read mind food that is part of the requirement of a successful individual.

Today I want you to start setting aside a place for all items that inspire you whether books, CDs, DVDs, videos and so on.

They might be nostalgic items or photographs from holidays or past events. Naturally I would hope this is where this book will live in the future, along with other books offering ideas to keep you achieving what you desire from your life.

Day 42

"People are where they are because that's exactly where they really want to be...whether they'll admit that or not." (William James)

A Further Reminder about Time

As we get further into the sixty days, here's another reminder about time. It's often being said that time feels like it's moving faster.

We do have a finite amount of this our most valuable commodity to use as we see fit until there's nothing left. As you read this book may I suggest now is a really good time to take stock of your life and appreciate the decisions you're making today will impact the results you achieve tomorrow.

So often we want to procrastinate with this wonderful idea that there's always time to do things that are not done yet... in the future. Though this might be the case to some extent, it would be a real disaster if you underestimated the time still available to you – in your very own time account. Today I ask you to think about something you've been putting off for a long time, to take action to do something towards it, or if it's feasible, complete on today!

Have you recently created a list of all the things that you've been meaning to do and not completed on? Today's about **completion**.

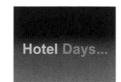

Time also for a Hotel Day

It's also time to go on a hotel day, either today or planned for a few days in advance. On your hotel day you will turn off your mobile phone and ideally let nobody know where you are headed.

When you get to your hotel you will find a place where you can sit and cogitate which would include brainstorming a review of days you've already completed on this journey and some planning for the future days and your ultimate achievements and ambitions. Hotel days can be remarkably successful.

Here are some suggestions on the structure of the day or half day:

- How far have I come since day one?
- What are my achievements to date?
- Am I passionate and motivated about my destination? Or should I make changes?
- Will I still get there by the planned deadline?
- Who is helping me get there or who else should I approach with this in mind?
- What more could I achieve on this journey if I knew I absolutely couldn't fail?
- How else do I make the most of my situation at the moment?
- How can I improve chances of success?

You're probably thinking – why do I need to book this in a hotel? Well you could choose an art gallery,

THE SIXTY DAY SUCCESS BLOG

restaurant, golf club, members' club or leisure centre. It's about getting away from familiar surroundings and being undisturbed.

So if you can't go today – book it in as soon as possible.

Day 43

"If the rate of change outside your team is greater than the rate of change inside your team, then the end is in sight." (Jack Welch)

Bringing the FUTURE into the present...

Living the Future in the Present

Many years ago it was suggested to me that I test drive the car that I most wanted to buy at the time. Of course the little voice in your head says, "If I don't have the funds to buy the car yet why on earth would I want to test drive it?" It's a bit like a friend of mine saying to me that she didn't like window shopping because she didn't have the money to buy all the things she wanted and therefore preferred not to see the items and thus as a result wouldn't miss what she didn't have the money to purchase.

This can be seen In two different ways. The first is where indeed you keep away from temptation by not going anywhere near the things you would dearly like to own. The second is by associating yourself and experiencing things you dearly wish to attain, interaction is going to speed the attainment much faster than if you were to ignore the images and experience.

When I approached my 30th birthday I decided to hire an Aston Martin for the weekend. Not necessarily having the spare money to hand at that exact moment in time I contacted the most local company I could find and paid down a deposit for the car, booking it for the weekend of my birthday. Once the booking was made I then set about making sure that the funds would be available when the time came to make the final payment.

That experience was one of the best birthday experiences in my life and I even hired my wedding photographer to capture the special moments that as a family we shared together.

Today I want you to look at how you can experience a little bit of what you ultimately want. For example you may wish to take a day off and experience freedom. The feeling of being able to get up when you want to without having to look at the clock and get to work and for the entire day feel how it feels to be financially independent running a life where you decide what you want to do.

If you'd love to live in a six-bedroom house overlooking the sea, why don't you make a point of going to 'test drive' one by ringing up an estate agent who could take you there.

These experiences are not pipedreams or living in 'cloud cuckoo land', they are opening your *reticular activation system* – that part of your brain which opens windows that currently could be closed.

When you open these windows in your mind, light shines through and you see the images of the things that are important to you. By experiencing these images regularly you are indeed more likely to ultimately see them by creating the result.

There's a story about T J Watson, founder of IBM, who set up the business in a small office which was a miniature of the big international global business he foresaw on day one of his venture. He made a point of hiring a secretary of extremely high quality in an office which equally, though small, was well decorated with some of the most expensive fixtures and fittings. He also went out and bought himself a suit which was five or six times more expensive than he would normally pay and all of this happened to coincide with day one starting his business. What was interesting by bringing the future into the present was that every person who met with him made the assumption that he was doing so well. He therefore attracted quality business and things moved very rapidly in the right direction and of course the rest is history. When you step into the future and see how it needs to be, then come back into the present, make the present as close to the future as possible, you are taking destiny into your own hands rather than let destiny push you around where you end up somewhere that unfortunately does not match your dreams and desires.

So today what could you do to bring the future into the present through a real experience?

Day 44

"Obstacles are those frightful things you see when you take your eyes off the goal." (Henry Ford)

What you Eat is who you are...

One of the classical links between brain and body through food is fish. Fish of course is well known for its health-giving properties and there's evidence to suggest that eating fish does you good in all sorts of ways. Today we're not simply talking fish; we're talking food in general. Write down what you ate yesterday from memory. When you've done that, make a list of what you intend to eat today.

Doing a quick analysis you should have three separate meals listed and if you're looking to be in good shape you might even consider up to six small meals a day. The content of your meals should be well balanced with plenty of attention on fruit, vegetables and a reasonable amount of water. I mention all of this because it's extraordinary how many people set sail for future success completely neglecting how they look after themselves. By the way your fair share of sleep also contributes to the house you live in called the human body.

Lunch is for wimps...

If you've ever seen the film 'Wall Street' with Michael Douglas you may remember the famous scene where he talks about lunch. "Lunch is for wimps", he said. That may be so in his world, but few performers – whether on the sports field or in the race for personal achievement – will make it by neglecting what food they eat and the amount of sleep they have.

Today is about checking diet and sleep. If these two health-connected items aren't where they should be, how can you maximise your potential in what you want to achieve?

The average human requires between 7 and 9 hours sleep a night. Having too much sleep is as bad as too little. Each person has their own amount they need. Be careful of telling yourself you can exist on 4 or 5 hours. Sure it can be done, but I'm not sure what shape you'll be in later on in your life. Your body is a delicate biological computer, and as we all know, computers also have a much needed 'sleep' option that will extend its machine life.

The time you put your head down is also relevant. Apparently 2200 hours is the ideal time to go to sleep if you like to wake early. Midnight and after may give you your seven hours, but it's likely to make you feel 'frayed at the edges' all the same.

So today work out what would work for you both in terms of regular healthy eating and sleep. It's not for me to go into the details here as I am your coach not a nutritionist. I am however keen that you look into this important area of personal development.

Day 45

"I can't think of anything worse than selling someone something they don't want." (Julian Richer – Richer Sounds)

Is your body a temple?

Is your body a temple?

Is your body a temple?

We will now look at exercise and health. Along any course of personal development and life improvement you may wish to consider how you're treating your temple or biological computer – the human body. There's the age-old adage about

computers namely *garbage in, garbage out*. This equates to what you programme in comes out as a result of the programme. Equally what you eat and what extent of the exercise you take will reflect on the quality of the body you inhabit.

I never understand people who neglect their body and yet want to be successful in their lives. What is the point of having monetary success if your health leaves a lot to be desired? Today I recommend you look into purchasing a copy of 'Body for Life' by Bill Phillips and Michael D'Orso.

If you're a member of a health club and you haven't been in a while, do yourself a favour and cancel your membership. I was speaking to someone at a health club recently where they have nearly one thousand members paying between £80 and £100 a month. They are also aware that only 322 people regularly attend the club every month! Great for the club, really sad for all the members who can't bring themselves to cancel because they think that cancelling will seriously ruin their chances of good health in the future... quite!

I'd also thoroughly recommend a personal trainer to a health club subscription, even if you do attend regularly. You will get a better return in less of the time where time is infinitely more valuable than money as we're all painfully aware. Today I suggest you sort your health out and at the very worst improve what you're doing to keep yourself in good shape.

Day 46

"We are what we repeatedly do. Excellence is not an act but a habit." (Aristotle)

The Research Day

If your goal(s) involve selling tangible things or intangible ideas to others you may wish to do some research on the competition today. By doing this, it's also likely to give you new ideas and help you improve your own prospects.

If your goal(s) do not relate to selling tangibles or intangibles, then I want you to choose something that you could sell. This would aid whatever else you wish to achieve as it will sharpen up your focus, approach and mental radar.

Things to look for in books or the Internet:

1. Who else has achieved what you wish to achieve? How did they do it?

2. Is there an alternative way to get to the finishing line for your goal(s)? It's great you want to climb this mountain, but what's most important, the climb or being on top? If it's the latter, have you checked if they have a cable car?

3. If you can't see others with what you want, what do others have that gets really close? How could you get closer or really close with your objective? (Based on the research on 'the competition').

Day 47

"People with clear, written goals accomplish far more in a shorter period of time than people without them could ever imagine." (Brian Tracy)

Skills based on Knowledge

Once again reach for a pad and a pen.

I would like you to write down one hundred words in one hundred and twenty seconds. However no word should contain the letter 'a'. Do this now and read no further as the ideal answer will be coming up.

Have you done it?

So how did you do? How many did you get? You may be interested to know that on average people who set out on this task get to around twenty-four items.

You may also be amused because it was much harder than you thought it would be. Did you get into the syndrome of thinking of a word and then rhyming it with as many letters as possible? I bet that didn't work as well as you were hoping! Unless you know the answer, which is about to come up, you probably feel quite disappointed with your result. It's true with anything that you wish to achieve; *the way you do it* is always the secret.

We all know that to create money from scratch you'd probably need to start with a job or sometimes an exceptional business idea that will work rapidly. Yet if most businesses fail in their first year and most individuals rarely hit the top of their career in the first twelve months, these methods cannot be the most effective.

The answer to writing down one hundred words as fast as possible without the letter 'a' would be: 1, 2, 3, 4, 5, 6, 7, 8, 9, 10, 11, 12, 13, 14, 15, 16, 17, 18, 19, 20... and so on right through to 100. None of these number words have the letter A in them!

That was rather simple wasn't it?

The fact is numbers are the quickest words to get down on paper because they follow a logical sequence which you first learned at around four years old. The answer was there all the time and there was you racking your brain to think of spurious words that didn't have the letter 'a' in them. So what's the point? Quite simply that skill is the steering wheel to knowledge.

How many extremely highly-qualified knowledgeable people are there out there in the world who are still making a pittance through lack of good skills? Millions.

There are three things that underpin successful people. You may remember these things by the word ASK:

**Attitude
+
Skill =
Knowledge**

Attitude + Skill = Knowledge.

This introduces the other element you should be aware of that's as powerful as skill and that's the attitude you carry in your head.

Whenever you want to do something ensure you engage the right attitude then seek out the skill you need and if necessary get trained up by somebody else who already possesses that skill.

Finally do some research and find out as much as you can to increase your knowledge appropriately. With all of these three things under your belt you become unstoppable.

Day 48

"Boldness has genius, magic and power in it. Begin it now." (Goethe)

Music – the motivator

Not all of us find music motivating and if music does nothing for you perhaps it might be an idea to move on to the next day or tell the little voice in your head to be quiet and have a go anyway.

The majority of people will always have at least one piece of music they are aware of that has a positive effect on them. For those of us who adore music, we will have countless music tracks that we regularly listen to that in turn affect us greatly.

Today, I'd like you to select one piece of music that you may wish to transfer to an iPod or keep handy on

THE SIXTY DAY SUCCESS BLOG

a CD that you play just once a day. Whenever you play it, I'd like you to create the most powerful images in your head of your current most desired goal in whatever you are doing right now. You'll also need some reminder mechanism so that you can do this at least for the next couple of weeks. So keep the CD near your bedside or in your car etc. It doesn't matter whether it's classical, jazz or pop. It's simply a piece of music that truly moves your soul every time you listen to it.

Day 49 *"We see the world not as it is but as we are." (Anon)*

That Special Place

For me there's a special place, a place of wondrous beauty which also has a small coffee shop that serves the most delicious Italian coffee.

I decided after a few visits to this place that I would only go there for inspiration. Do you have anywhere like this in your life? Think about it because if you haven't, it's time you found somewhere. The idea of this place is not about spending vast amounts of time there, just the odd moment or half an hour or twenty minutes where you can recharge your batteries and hopefully take away a couple of ideas you didn't have when you walked in.

It might take you some time to investigate where this special place could possibly be and there's nothing to stop you changing your special place location from time to time so that the inspiration is always there. I know for me that if I need some inspiration in a hurry and I'm relatively close to my home or office, there's a place I can head to and as I make my way there I will already start to feel better. To date I've also always come away with an idea that has made the trip entirely worthwhile. So where is your place? If you don't have one, find it today? Then visit it. If you have no time for the visit, diarise when you can go.

Day 50

"It's choice not chance that determines your destiny."
(Anthony Robbins)

Today I must tell you about a very simple habit that has enormous potential in terms of wins and rewards. I call it the '4-call-a-day habit'.

I fully appreciate that this could equally be a three call a day habit and for some reason in my experience four calls have had the best result for me which is why it's a strong recommendation. The way you incorporate this habit into your daily routine is to ensure that every day you make four calls to four separate people whom you haven't spoken to in a while. I normally gauge this on someone I've not spoken to for at least thirty days, though sometimes I notice I have people on my list who I've not spoken to for years!

For the system to work you should not underpin the decision to ring someone based on an evaluation of what might or might not happen on the call. Should you run out of names, you should select complete strangers from friends of friends, people you are aware of or indeed individuals who've made the newspapers recently for something positive they've achieved.

The 4-call-a-day idea can produce quite simply the most staggering results. In reality this is akin to an NPR call. NPR stands for no particular reason and it's when you ring someone you know for no particular reason that they relax and the discussion becomes quite fluid, flexible and very often supportive and helpful to you. What I usually tend to do is speak very positively about what I'm currently doing in my life and there's no surprise when their offers of help to assist you further along the way arise.

So today I would like you to set up your 4-call-a-day system by creating a log entry so that from now on every day you have the four people you've listed and their phone numbers. This will also help you in terms of knowing when it's time to ring them again.

What's also good about this system is that if you make the call and you get through to someone's voicemail, by leaving a message you have completed the call. When the person rings you back the following day however that conversation is not one of the calls for that day. You still have to make four separate calls.

If right now there's no particular need to do this level of networking, it is acceptable to do this with less calls, even a single call a day, as there will be benefits all the same. If you really want to make life successful use the 4-call-a-day system and only pare back on the number if things are going swimmingly well for you already.

Day 51

"Seek to understand before being understood." (Stephen Covey)

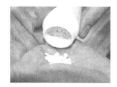

Today I read an amazing article about the placebo effect. In medicine placebos are used alongside other 'real' drugs in trials to test efficacy of the treatment. So for example a new drug is trialled with six patients and alongside this trial six other patients will be given placebos or tablets which have no curative effect on the patient with the same disease. The fascinating part about such tests is that sometimes, in fact more often than you would suppose, those receiving placebos get equally good results as those receiving the 'real' drug. There are also occasions when those receiving placebos get better sooner than those receiving the pucker treatment. This then is the placebo effect in action. Curious that science cannot actually explain why placebos work other than it's 'all in the mind'. What many physicians are afraid of admitting is that the human mind can cure its counterpoint body by thinking the right thoughts. If this isn't inspiring enough for you to think about today and then link it to some of the things you want to achieve in your own life – things that are not working that need dealing with – consider something else in addition.

During trials with placebos in a hospital specialising in cardiac operations, they put half the patients in rooms that looked out on red brick walls and the other half of the patients in rooms that overlooked trees, foliage and open parkland. The evidence of patients getting well sooner and leaving the hospital in a smaller time frame is quite staggering. These patients had all spent their post-operative time recuperating in the latter room with trees and open space to look onto. Once again, those scientists will not admit it officially. What we see through our eyes does affect our minds and has a really strong influence on what we process through our brain and how those stimuli and responses affect our entire being, behaviour and ultimately health.

How is your home or office set up? What do you look onto? If you have a desk facing into a wall, have you not thought of turning it around so you have your back to the wall and you look into the room, and if you have the opportunity of looking out of the window to a great view isn't it time you really maximised on this catalyst for success?

Today is about looking at how you are set up at home and/or your office and what changes you might make to improve your chances of better outcomes.

Day 52

"A life spent making mistakes is not only more honourable, but more useful than a life spent doing nothing." (George Bernard Shaw)

I sat and read an account recently by a top American entrepreneur. In this article he made a very simple statement which resonated with me and something I would very much like to share with you.

When you do some work in your life would you not prefer to do it once and be paid for that work again and again in the future? Isn't it true that for most of us we do the complete opposite? We set ourselves up in a situation, often called a job, where the work that we do has to be repeated again and again for us to be paid. If we stop doing the work we stop getting paid.

So what work would fall in the former category where you do it the once and get paid for evermore? Here are a few to choose from:

- Royalties on books
- Royalties on music
- Commissions on introduced business

- Rental incomes
- Anything you sell at a subscription which is ongoing

It's all too easy to dismiss this list of things and say, "I'm not in these marketplaces" yet surely this is a personal choice. If you want to capitalise on an opportunity that will make your life so much more easy to live and more effective in terms of creating wealth, then you should really spend today using a mind map and doing some mind blasting around how you can reshape some if not all of your income based on these bullet points. This is your mission for today.

Day 53   *"Start with the end in mind." (Stephen Covey)*

Enjoying the Moment

In our busy lives when we rush around from one thing to the next what we fail to realise is that the moments of life that we live we cannot live again.

Every minute every second is spent the moment we think about it, though there is one saving grace, setting up the process of **enjoying the moment.**

To enjoy the moment more, you need to make this a habit. You may wish to remind yourself about the whole matter by putting the reminder on an index card and reading this every day. Enjoying the moment can be a challenge at times because there will be things that you're challenged by that quite frankly you're not enjoying at all. And the more you enjoy on a regular basis, the more you will enjoy your life by enjoying every piece of it that is possible to enjoy.

Often I've been accused of being miles away at a family dinner for example because my mind is not on the present it's on what I'm supposed to be doing tomorrow in the office or what I should be saying to a particular client.

To really make this work in your life and to enjoy your life more, you may have to put a lot of reminders around you to start with and once you get into the habit you will start to really not only enjoy your life but also appreciate that it slows down which is not a bad thing given that as we grow older time itself tends to speed up even though we can do things to prevent this. Forcing yourself to enjoy the moment is one such thing.

Day 54

"You cannot control what happens to you but you can control your attitude toward what happens to you, and in that, you will be mastering change rather than allowing it to master you." (Brian Tracy)

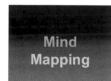

Mind mapping

I've mentioned mind maps and there are some at the back of the book. Today I want you to explore mind maps some more. If you already use them, then simply mind map where you are so far on your journey and I'll catch you tomorrow.

For everyone else, consider this...linear thinking has very little value when you want your life to expand, grow and thrive whichever direction you choose for it. I've long understood the power of mind maps invented by Tony Buzan. These can be done freehand or using his mind mapping software to great effect. You may be aware that there are two sides of the brain – right and left – where the right is largely creative and the left is apparently logical and analytical. As I write this I do appreciate that there are some men and women of science who do not fully agree with this very distinct differentiation. For my purposes I'm going to assume that this is largely true and in any event doesn't affect the outcome of my message today. So mind mapping is about being more creative and creativity is always the vantage point in life's game of tennis.

You will see the use of mind maps at the end of this book and I want to record a few basic notes of how you should create them.

- Have a central theme on the page where the page is landscape.
- Use plenty of colour.
- Emanating from the centre theme should be branches, preferably of different colours, where each branch is a subject of the main theme.

- Branches break into smaller extremities and often the branch is described as the parent and the smaller extremity, the child stem of thinking.
- Write along the branches or extremities in succinct language where less is more.
- Add pictures or diagrams alongside your branches and notes to make the page highly visual and easy to follow with the eye.

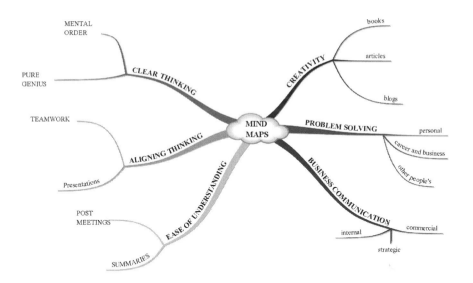

You don't have to be too artistic to draw a great mind map just simply be prepared to think simplicity not complexity. As we grow older we tend to become more complex and complicated in our thinking which is often lost in reams of linear notes which are difficult to reread apart from looking very boring. Today you need to explore mind maps and start to use them without any further delay. There is much you can look at on the Internet referencing the work of Tony Buzan.

Day 55

"If you work just for money, you'll never make it, but if you love what you're doing and you always put the customer first, success will be yours." (Arthur Kroc)

I'm very interested in the speed and growth in technological advancement today. There are many people on the planet who have become overnight millionaires and success stories by getting to grips with technology and using it to create huge advantage in just about every industry that exists.

Whatever your industry or career path, technology used in the right way can not only enhance what you do, it can give you distinct competitive advantage. This relates to running a business or being part of a corporate where climbing the ladder of success is very much on your mind as an important ambition for your future.

You are already familiar with YouTube. How about Facebook and other free sites where you can network or download information? For example there's also MySpace and eBay which have helped to make people very successful overnight.

Today I want you to contact somebody who has used any of these for personal advantage and ask them to explain to you how these sites work if you are unfamiliar with them.

If you are familiar with them, I want to ask you to make some money using any one of them. The challenge is to make £100 in the next seventy-two hours. I presume you're probably going to go for eBay which is the obvious quick return site and if you have never done this before and can make £100 in seventy-two hours I am pretty sure you will be inspired to take this further. No doubt you're aware that there are countless people the world over whose primary pursuit in life is a full-time business opportunity using sites like eBay.

Day 56

"How am I going to live today in order to create the tomorrow I'm committed to." (Anthony Robbins)

The Brains Trust

Many decades ago there was a radio programme on the BBC called something *The Brains Trust*.

Here you had a group of highly successful and knowledgeable individuals who would be asked all sorts of questions by a studio audience. What I'd like you to consider is to create your own brains trust with people that you know.

My suggestion is that you form this group of individuals and meet collectively at least once a month for a couple of hours. The purpose of meeting is for each of

THE SIXTY DAY SUCCESS BLOG

you to be able to ask three questions of the other people in the room and get some considered answers for your evaluation. It's true that we tend to be able to answer the questions, challenges and problems of other people more easily than doing it for ourselves. Also a problem or question shared is a problem or question halved. This stands to reason. You should have a minimum of three people in your brains trust with a maximum of six. I challenge you today to create your own brains trust and pencil in your first meeting in a few weeks from now. Even if you only ever meet once, I promise you it will be a worthwhile activity. There is much to gain from such a unity of potentially highly creative thinking.

Day 57

"For the things we have to learn before we can do them, we learn by doing them." (Aristotle)

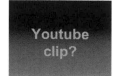

Today I need you to look at YouTube again.

We've already established that there's a vast amount of knowledge that you can obtain for free on

YouTube. If that's not a reason enough to visit it regularly from time to time to see what's there, you should also consider uploading clips that would help you in what you want to achieve.

Grab a video camera or mobile phone with a video facility and record two or three messages that you'd be willing to upload on YouTube today.

There's no question that the better the quality of the clip the more chances are that the right people will view it. But in terms of the sixty-day success blog, the critical factor is to get something uploaded today as your commitment to achieving success. You may easily improve on your clip in due course, though I do want you to take some action today.

There are two publications you may wish to consider *The Writer's Handbook* and *the Writers' and Artists' Year Book.*

These reference guides will tell you the market for writing in the United Kingdom and other parts of the world. The reason why they are worth referencing and are obtainable in most libraries, is so that you could consider writing an article for a journal that would help you attract help, support, interest and custom as required linked to your ambitions.

If you don't have any ambitions that require some publicity, then do this all the same to prove that you are a good and effective communicator which is equally important.

How to write a good article:

- Use a mind map to explore content
- Make the paragraphs short, sharp and punchy
- Provide photographic material where possible
- Write a preliminary letter first without the article to check interest from the publisher
- Do discuss a fee – as you're worth it!

Do have a good header which attracts people's interest to read the piece in the first place

- Always use a spell checker before you send off your work
- Don't be afraid to use the telephone and ring up the publication and ask to speak to someone

about the possibility of your article being accepted

Articles can be as little as one hundred words and there's really no excuse to doing this as your first journey into creative writing for your personal short, medium and long-term achievement.

Day 58

"If you don't know where you are going, every road will get you nowhere." (Henry Kissinger)

We are but three days away from the end of our journey. If you've taken action each day on the tasks I have set out for you, you will have experienced three things. One, a learning experience from the task. Secondly, a catalyst that will help you attain success through focusing on your goals and, thirdly, the attainment of a powerful but little-used habit by most would-be goal achievers – *taking action!*

So if you've taken action on each daily chunk, I know you've already had some amazing breakthroughs. If you haven't, then there are two reasons. Firstly, you are simply reading the book, not following the instructions. That's not how this book's designed. Blogs are normally daily messages like a diary. So I would ask you to go back to day one and start again. If you want a guaranteed outcome, this is the only way I know you can attain everything you desire.

Secondly, if you've not had any breakthroughs yet, it means you've cheated! You can't pick and choose each day. You can't do days 3, 12 and 17 onwards because you like and approve of these ones... It's all or nothing.

So if you've done what I suggested – you will be on a high today, and I say, congratulations, put your feet up today and have a few moments savouring the new you. A goal-focused, action-orientated achiever who, by virtue of this fact, can go out into the world and achieve, just about anything!

If you're not in this happy position yet, then you know what you must do. If you do it, I predict success for you. Now ask yourself the question: what will I have by *not doing it?*

Day 59

"I must create a system, or be enslaved by another man's." (William Blake)

Chicken Call Day

You've already been asked to proactively make a call or two. Now let's really roll up our sleeves.

If you are doing your FOUR CALLS A DAY, one call must now be a chicken call,

A chicken call is where you know who you'd love to speak to and who would help you and yet are afraid to call.

It might be someone extremely famous or simply somebody you know who you'd love to connect with but can never summon up the courage to pick up the phone, dial their number and speak with them.

The first part of this process is to write down all the people you would love to connect with. Who knows you may wish to put Richard Branson at the top of the list! Though it doesn't matter who you list, but you

THE SIXTY DAY SUCCESS BLOG

should think about appropriate people. For example I'm sure it would be wonderful to be able to prospect a member of the Cabinet and for them to take your call but if you have no real purpose in doing this, I'm sure from both points of view it's going to be a very short conversation assuming you got through.

And this is an important point. If you have a real desire to get to speak to someone for a really good reason you're more likely to make that breakthrough.

The surprising thing about putting in a call to someone who you assume would not want to speak to you is that of every ten you put in at least two of them would definitely converse with you and probably one of the two would be able to do something for you. Like many other things in this book, this is yet another idea that does request taking action and following through with boldness that we all possess and yet don't wish to deploy.

I remember the first time I attempted a chicken call and it was a famous sporting celebrity. I left two or three messages with his secretary to call me back and lo and behold (I shouldn't really have been surprised should I), he did indeed call back. We had a conversation and though I didn't quite get the outcome I hoped for it really helped inspire me to greater things.

So who are you going to call?

Day 60

"Do not go where the path may lead, go instead where there is no path and leave a trail." (Ralph Waldo Emerson)

Congratulations if you've reached the finishing line having taken things day by day and completed on all your daily tasks.

Today is about celebrating your achievement. Acknowledging that success isn't difficult or obscure. It's not meant for certain personalities, lucky groups of people or a chosen few.

Success is about taking things in bite-size chunks, applying a few simple rules, using simple easy-to acquire-skills, and then proactively taking control, accepting personal responsibility, and with the right mindset, making the right moves in the right direction. That's what the 60-day Success Blog was created for. And if you've followed the instructions you should join me now toasting the new successful you.

I contend that we were all born successful, it's just that most of us have overlooked the fact. We've grown up in a world where the messages we receive centre around what's wrong, not what's right, what we don't have, not what we do, and who we're not rather than who we really are.

Here's hoping that you also realise that your journey's not at an end, it's only just truly begun. You have the rest of your life and all of your dreams yet to fulfil. Your future awaits you.

Every success!

Resources

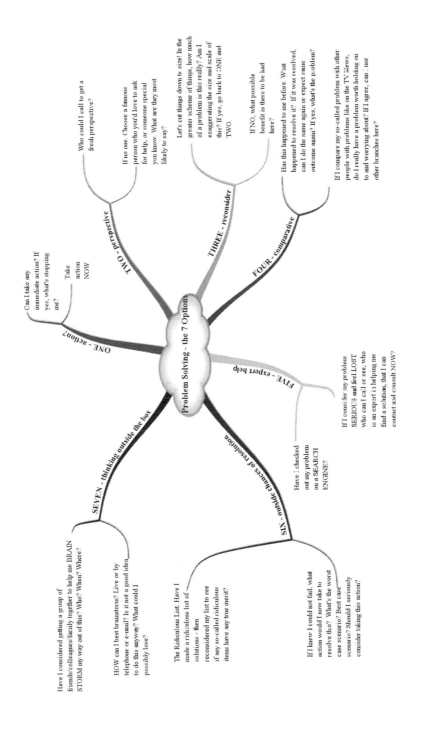

Problem Solving - the 7 Options

ONE - action?
- Can I take any immediate action? If yes, what's stopping me?
- Take action NOW

TWO - perspective
- Who could I call to get a fresh perspective?
- If no one. Choose a famous person who you'd love to ask for help, or someone special you know. What are they most likely to say?

THREE - reconsider
- Let's cut things down to size! In the greater scheme of things, how much of a problem is this really? Am I exaggerating the size and scale of this? If yes, go back to ONE and TWO.
- If NO, what possible benefit is there to be had here?

FOUR - comparative
- Has this happened to me before. What happened to resolve it? If it was resolved, can I do the same again or expect same outcome again? If yes, what's the problem?
- If I compare my so-called problem with other people with problems like on the TV news, do I really have a problem worth holding on to and worrying about? If I agree, can I use other branches here?

FIVE - expert help
- If I consider my problem SERIOUS and feel LOST who can I call or see, who is an expert in helping me find a solution, that I can contact and consult NOW?

SIX - possible choices of resolution
- Have I checked out my problem on a SEARCH ENGINE?
- If I knew I could not fail, what action would I now take to resolve this? What's the worst case scenario? Best case scenario? Should I seriously consider taking this action?
- The Ridiculous List. Have I made a ridiculous list of solutions – then reconsidered my list to see if any so-called ridiculous items have any true merit?

SEVEN - thinking outside the box
- HOW can I best brainstorm? Live or by telephone or e-mail? Is it not a good idea to do this anyway? What could I possibly lose?
- Have I considered getting a group of friends/colleagues/family together to help me BRAIN STORM my way out of this? Who? When? Where?

I'm STUCK!

Ask your subconscious

Write what you need to get unstuck on a card. Read it before you go to bed. Leave the card by your bed. Do this three nights in a row. The chances are you'll have the answer in 72 hours!

WHAT IF?

Write down your top 3 what if questions. So if you being stuck was someone else and not you... what 3 what if questions are you most likely to ask to get them unstuck?

WHAT resource would help me?

What resource are you missing? Consider the Internet, a big book store, your own book collection, a library, AMAZON, university resources you could tap into. Other people's resources? (Who?)

WHO would have an answer?

Who do you know that is most likely to give you an answer right now?

Blank paper, pen and ON interruptions

Be in a place where there are three things going on. ONE - you have a blank sheet of paper. TWO - you have a pen (preferably a set of coloured pens) and THREE - no mobile phone, or communication device.

Change your location

Often a change of location makes a big difference on your thought process - leave your current location and head for somewhere that you'd feel good about...

Check out PROBLEM SOLVING

If this being stuck is more of a problem stopping you - look at the Problem Solving Mind Map.